AKASHIC RECORDS

A Spiritual Journey to Accessing the Center of Your Universal Soul, Master Your Life Purpose, and Raise Your Vibrations

Melissa Gomes

Akashic Records: A Spiritual Journey to Accessing the Center of Your Universal Soul, Master Your Life Purpose, and Raise Your Vibrations

by Melissa Gomes

TABLE OF CONTENTS

BONUS: FREE AUDIO VERSION

OF THIS BOOK

If you love listening to audiobooks on-the-go or would enjoy a narration as you read along, I have great news for you. You can download the audiobook version of **this book** for FREE just by signing up for a FREE 30-day Audible trial!

VISIT THE FOLLOWING LINK:

https://swiy.io/AkashicRecordsAudio

OR scan the QR code with your phone:

Bonus: Free Workbook - Value $~~$12.99~~

To help you take some time for yourself and reflect on what actions to take while reading the book, I have prepared a Free Workbook with some key questions to ask yourself and a To Do List which can help you get deeper into the topic of this book. I hope this helps!

You can find the Free Workbook by visiting
>> https://swiy.io/AkashicRecordsMGWorkbook<<

OR scan the QR Code with your phone's camera

BONUS: FREE BOOK – VALUE

~~$14.99~~

As a way of saying thank you for downloading this book, I'm offering the eBook *RUNES FOR BEGINNERS A Pagan Guide to Reading and Casting the Elder Futhark Rune Stones for Divination, Norse Magic, and Modern Witchcraft* for FREE.

In *Runes for Beginners*, Melissa Gomes reveals some of the most interesting and secret aspects of how to perform Runes Reading and Runes Casting. You will discover new insights into the magical word of Runes and how to link with them.

Click Below for the Free Gift OR Scan the QR Code with your phone

INTRODUCTION

The Akashic Records are the records of all human thoughts, words and deeds that have ever existed. It's a myth that only highly intelligent people are creative. In fact, research shows that once you get beyond an I.Q. of about 120, which is just a little above average. Even though intelligent people might have a little advantage, intelligence is not required for creativity. That means that even if you're no smarter than most people, you still have the potential to wield amazing creative powers. So why are so few people highly creative? Because there are bad habits people learn as they grow up which crush the creative pathways in the brain. And like all bad habits, they can be broken if you're willing to work at it." Here's 8 of those bad habits which must be dropped to unleash your creative powers.

#1: Work for money. Wouldn't it be wonderful if we could get rich without having to struggle? Wouldn't it also be wonderful if life were simpler, and indeed easier, so that we didn't have to worry as much about material things? In other words, what would the world be like if we didn't have to work?

Well, it wouldn't be heaven, but there would be some significant advantages. The important thing to realize is that working for money is an option you can choose not to do. As long as we're alive, we can't avoid some work. As Walt Disney said, "All our dreams can come true - if we have the courage to pursue them." You don't want to just dream about money - you want to find an easier way of getting it so you can spend your time doing something more creative!

#2: Don't take responsibility for your life. You can be a victim of the circumstances around you, or you can make some changes and take charge of the direction your life will go. This is really where creativity comes in – if you don't like what's happening to you, then change it! As Merlin Mann said, "Happiness doesn't come from getting what you want, it comes from wanting what you get. "

#3: Don't have goals. What do people mean when they say that someone is "directionless?" That's a code word for lack of productivity – in other words, the person isn't doing anything important with his or her life because he or she doesn't have a clear idea of where he or she is going. It's no different than driving somewhere without having a map – you'll eventually end up lost! The solution? Decide what it is you want, and then decide how to get there."

#4: Don't accept rejection. Rejection can break people, but it doesn't have to. For example, if you've ever been turned down for a job you wanted, or rejected by someone you were attracted to romantically, then you know how painful it can be. The key is not to take it personally – just accept that "that's the way the cookie crumbles" and get back on track."

5: Don't take action. The first principle of creativity is that you have to get started! Stop thinking and talking - just do it! There will always be obstacles in your path, but if you don't make a move, then where are you going? You'll never know what great thing might result from taking a chance on something, but you will know if you don't."

#6: Don't take help. We hear all the time about someone who "did it on their own," and how that's a good thing. That may be true, but only up to a point. The problem with not accepting help is that it deprives you of all that other people know. If you want to be creative you also have to be open-minded about taking ideas from other people – that's how all great innovations happen! "When an artist dips his pen in his inkpot, he is then and there responsible for what he does with it," said Leonardo da Vinci."

#7: Don't learn from others. Of course, you have to find out all you can about what you want to do – but there's one important caveat: don't let your learning process be a passive experience. You must get out there and do some things on your own! That's how you'll come up with your own creative ideas, instead of thinking you have to reinvent the wheel."

#8: Don't be spontaneous. Seeming out of control is scary – but it shouldn't be. If people think that you're going crazy, then they won't understand the power of your creativity. They'll simply think you've lost it and are no longer a safe person for them to deal with. To manage people's reactions, you need to build a reputation for being "together."

By taking control of your life and career, by using the principles in this book to get where you want to go, you'll be seen as a person who is reasonable and safe – even if what is really going on inside you is totally different!

This book should help you in your journey in opening your Akashic Records to be able to use them for your benefit. It will help you grasp what they are and how to access and understand the information stored in them.

We believe that knowing who you are is important, especially when it comes to using the Akashic Records, and so we have created this guide to teach you just that. With a little practice you will be able to access your very own Akashic Records in no time at all.

CHAPTER 1. UNLOCKING THE SECRETS OF READING AKASHIC RECORDS

Have you ever witnessed an immense amount of light that such light can feel heady to average humans? You can get a glimpse of this light and enter a state of full rapture. This state occurs due to the amount of divine energy you are subjected to. This light is your Akashic Records. When you read your Records, you should feel more in sync with your soul and the divine nature surrounding you.

WHAT ARE AKASHIC RECORDS?

The Akashic Records are a collection of all that's known, unknown, and unknowable. They contain information about you, your soul, and everything else in the universe. The good news is they also offer a process to connect with the divine knowing of your soul at this moment. When someone opens your akashic records, for example, you have access to both information about yourself and knowledge from the divine source of all beingness within this moment.

What you get from the Akashic Records is always in response to the questions you ask. They will answer the questions as simply or complexly as you desire, depending on your level of interest.

The Akashic Records are also a storehouse of knowledge about our past lives and lifetimes on Earth. The Records hold information about the soul's journey on Earth as well as in other lifetimes. They contain a history of the evolution and growth of souls over millions of years, details unknown or unimagined by conventional scholars.

For entry into the Akashic Records, I follow a straightforward procedure that includes a vision and blessing. The procedure, which is similar to other traditions, allows you to ask questions of the Akashic Records and receive answers that are accurate, detailed, and relevant.

What do I mean by a blessing? The blessing is an introduction between your open mind and divine source within the greater reality at this moment. Therefore, it starts with acknowledging your higher self, your connection to the divine source of all beingness that is always within you and everything else in the universe.

With this powerful connection as a foundation, your conscious mind can get answers from the divine source of all knowledge. With your blessing, questions are asked to the Records with confidence on behalf of an open mind. The answers don't require faith or belief. They are the divine knowing of your soul now; therefore, they are intuitively obvious and immutably true.

Raising your good vibrations to a high level and experiencing spiritual awakening will improve your life. It will help you manifest what is most meaningful for you in life, make your decisions more easily, and strengthen the bond between you and your soul. For these reasons, it is important to enter into the Akashic Records whenever you're curious about anything in life.

Even if they include future outcomes, the Records are not designed like a fortuneteller. The Akashic Records reflect people's own choices and decisions throughout their lives—as well as our souls' choices in other lifetimes. The element of choice is really important to know because it means we are all creators. When you realize that decisions shape your life, you can look at the past and anticipate the future with more awareness about what to do next.

The Akashic Records may be accessed consistently and repeatedly for guidance in many areas of life. You can ask questions about anything—health, relationships, career, money matters, spiritual growth—and receive accurate and detailed information about the past and guidance for the future.

The Records can also be used to look into your own past lives and times on Earth that have special meaning for you. They are like a cosmic history book of our soul's evolution throughout time. You may find it interesting to know that many people who experience readings from their Records report having out-of-body experiences, astral travel, or near-death experiences (NDE).

At first, it might seem odd to think that souls can incarnate in many lifetimes in different places across the globe. But if you consider that your soul has been around since before, we were all living here at one time, perhaps memories of other places and past lifetimes are all part of the greater experience of who you are.

WHERE ARE THE AKASHIC RECORDS STORED?

The Akashic Records are thought to exist in an ethereal, non-physical plane known as the "Akasha." The Akasha flows through everything in our universe. It flows through nature, matter, and our souls. The Akasha encompasses everything. However, the Akashic Records do not give you any physical power like telekinesis.

The Akashic Records are also thought by many to be a collective consciousness or a more primal form of collective unconsciousness. This means that memories are stored in our world as energy patterns, and these energy patterns are molded into forms and objects by our thoughts and emotions. Our thoughts and emotions have evolved through natural selection, but they still influence reality today. We can say that such things as DNA strands store imprints of past lives, which we can access when receiving readings from the Records.

Many believe the Records exist in other dimensions outside of ours because it is part of an ethereal plane where all possible realities exist simultaneously (past, present, future). It is thought that our souls have a direct connection to the Akashic Records through out-of-body experiences, astral travel, and NDEs. The information found in the Records often makes sense when it's interpreted, which is why many people believe they are authentic. Since information can be obtained by accessing other dimensions through these experiences, we can also obtain knowledge about former lives just as easily.

Because of its ethereal nature, there are no physical locations where this database is stored; however, you can access it from any location at any time – from your own room or even while dreaming – as long as your consciousness is aware of being within the Akasha. Some speculate it exists beyond Earth, in other galaxies or universes, such as the Gaia Soul. There are no limits to where it exists and where we can access it as beings of consciousness (souls).

The ether or Akashic Records within our reality are made up of information that has been organized into layers or levels, which you must train your soul to experience after obtaining instruction in accessing them. It's recommended that one should practice connecting with their Akashic Record before time traveling through astral planes, hard-wired networks when accessing blank spots of times throughout history, including parallel universes for predicting future events.

You can also use a crystal ball, scrying mirror, or an enchanted mirror to access your Akashic Records. Still, it's recommended one works with a trained spiritual medium for this type of activity. Reading the Records will help you unveil and understand yourself by discovering events in your past lives. You may also be able to obtain information about future lifetimes or parallel dimensions, including what parts you play in them affecting world affairs.

Adventurers curious about their soul's origins can even travel through esoteric portal systems beyond space and time to observe various historical periods throughout our universe and others where we are known as star seeds, wanderers, extraterrestrials, aliens, and more. Some of us enjoy these travels more than living on Earth because life there is so unpredictable.

Akashic Records: The Origins

The origins of the Akashic Records are not known for sure, but it is believed that their modern beginning was in the 1800s in Europe. Many people began to learn about Hinduism and Buddhism due to the transmission of ideas that started through the British colonization of India in the late 1700s.

The British were interested in India for trade and natural resources, and military prowess to protect their homeland from other European colonial powers. During this time, there was a great deal of cross-cultural exchange with the Hindu culture. Therefore, many people began to learn different spiritual approaches. It seems that at this time, the British began to learn about Hinduism and Buddhism in India.

During this time, many raised Christian people began to feel that there was more to life than what they had learned from Christianity. They wanted something more spiritual and relevant to their everyday lives. This is when many Europeans first heard of the mystical teachings of Eastern religions.

In the early 1800, there was an explosion of interest in spirituality and Eastern religions. This happened for two reasons. First, people felt a need to understand more about their spiritual natures than what Christianity had taught them. Second, many Europeans began traveling to Asia and learning from books about Hinduism and Buddhism.

The Akashic Records began to be talked about in Western Europe and North America. This was the beginning of a new era that included scientific research, political revolutions, great discoveries, and social changes with industrialization. At this time, people started to talk about keeping spiritual records such as the Akashic Records for recording the history of the soul.

The Sumerian civilization in the Mesopotamian area. was located between the Tigris and Euphrates Rivers in what is now Iraq. A hint to the Akashic Records was found in the ancient Mesopotamian concept of the Tablet of Destinies. The Tablet of Destinies and the Book of Life, were two tablets: one for good and one for evil omens. These tablets represented divine knowledge and recorded events during a lifetime that were destined to happen from birth to death.

The records were believed to have been kept by the gods, who determined destiny and fate in advance. They wrote down the information about an individual's life on these tablets before they were born. Then they sealed them in front of witnesses as a kind of proof of future events.

Then the tablets were buried in a temple where they would be kept safe and secret until the person's death. They could be opened, and it was believed that the truth about what had happened during their life would be written inside. To find out more about their life story, it seems that an individual could be taken to the temple and shown the tablets. After reading them, they would read their personal life story from beginning to end.

DO YOU NEED ANY SPECIFIC POWER TO ACCESS THE AKASHIC RECORDS?

No, it is not the power of any one person. It just takes an open mind and a little bit of patience for you to see that this spiritual dimension exists.

Nowadays, anyone can read their Akashic Records. In fact, you may even know somebody who has done this and come back feeling less afraid of the world because they know that what happened before will happen again in a different form. This helps people feel better prepared when dealing with change in their lives.

Furthermore, it might be easier than you think to have access to your Records as long as you are willing to try new ways of reading your past lives by tapping into our natural psychic abilities. Psychic abilities can be developed with regular practice and patience.

No, you do not need any supernatural power to access your Akashic Records; however, some people who have had such gifts from birth may indeed use them instinctively. Nevertheless, anyone can do this by developing the essential skill of open-mindedness and trust. Therefore, there are no prerequisites to be able to read your Akashic Records.

However, what you may find is that reading the Akashic Records can appear to be a bit strange at first, and it may take time for you to become accustomed to the sensation of remembering a lifetime as if you are living it.

What techniques can be used to access the Akashic Records?
As we progress through life, we interact with it constantly, and thus, all of our experiences are stored somehow. Our brains function as a storage device for these experiences, but this does not mean that our memories and emotions are imprinted on the physical brain.

There is something else out there besides the physical realm. In addition to the physical universe, there is also a spiritual dimension. There are other ways for us to think about and perceive ourselves and our world.

Journaling is one helpful technique in accessing your Akashic Records because it allows you to start thinking of a positive change in your life by looking into the future. It is a simple technique because all you have to do is write down your thoughts and feelings about how you think life will be in the future or even in the distant past.

By doing this, you are permitting yourself to access information about yourself that you might not normally remember. Once you discipline yourself to journal regularly, you will find that your journals become sources of information about what you have done in the past and where you need to go.

Running can also help you tap into memories from previous lifetimes (by tapping into the physical space between you and other people, therefore becoming one with it), as running mimics our natural movement while living our last lifetime. In addition, you can help yourself remember a past life by drawing things that remind you of the experience in your current life.

It is difficult to tell exactly how much time it takes for most people to see positive results from using these techniques because they all respond differently and change at different paces; however, it is a common trend that people see results within a few weeks of using these techniques consistently.

THE MEANING OF "AKASHIC"

The word "Akashic" is derived from the Sanskrit word Akasha, which means "ether" or "sky." In fact, ether is an important Physical substance or subtle substance in Hinduism. It is said to be the "energy" of all things.

Ether is the substance that fills space between objects and being around those objects without touching them. It is known to be a subtle omnipresent substance that lies in the background of our existence. Ether can hold energy and does not give it off or absorb it easily.

Akasha is another word that means "sky." Akasha carries several different meanings. One of them relates to the space between and above planets, stars, and galaxies. Another meaning comes from the Sanskrit language, where it has several shades of meaning, including "ancient matter", "avenue to heaven" and "heavens"

This term has been used to describe a universal record of all that ever was, is, and will be and a record of past and future lives.

SPIRITUAL ENERGY

The word "akasha" is also used in Sanskrit to describe spiritual energy, which permeates and surrounds us with its luminous light. This radiates from the spirit outward into surrounding space, which is called the aura.

When tapped by man, Akasha contains latent spiritual energy and can be used to heal or for other purposes. The Heart Chakra (Anahata) - located in the center of the chest - represents our emotional heart and seat of unconditional love. It plays an important role in tapping into and using akashic energy.

In Hinduism, it refers to an ethereal substance from which everything in existence emanates and into which it returns at death; this includes both living beings and inanimate objects.

It also refers to a spiritual plane of existence where one's life records are kept before being reincarnated back on Earth. It is also believed to be the repository of all knowledge.

This elementary substance is considered a medium for transmitting radio waves, ultraviolet rays, and visible light. A related word, Akasha Ganga, means "river of ethereal space." This refers to an invisible essence found within our solar system and galaxy that permeates all matter and energy.

DIVINE IDEAS

The word "akasha" can also refer to a field of divine ideas containing every form, pattern, and concept that exists. These are the "blueprints" for everything that is now or will ever be created in our universe.

This field is sort of like a cosmic library (library of knowledge) where every book has been written and can be read by those who have the ability to do so. In this context, "akasha" means a field or medium through which information is transmitted and received. It also indicates the space between objects where energy can be stored and/or transmitted.

THE MAIN BENEFITS OF READING THE AKASHIC RECORDS

RAISING YOUR GOOD VIBRATIONS

When reading the Akashic Records and raising your good vibrations, you will be able to eliminate any self-defeating thoughts that might be holding you back from living a fulfilling life. You'll also learn how to respond more positively in all situations by looking for the higher meaning in anything that happens. Raising your vibrations can lead to radical awakening and will result in a much better future. In fact, when reading the Akashic Records, you can be assured that your highest good will always come from it.

What is the highest good? When raising your vibrations and fulfilling your true destiny, all of our actions must be for our highest good and, as a result, to better others in some way.

RECEIVING SPIRITUAL ENERGY

When reading the Akashic Records, you'll be able to tap into a field of Divine Ideas, which contain every pattern, form, and concept that has ever existed. These are the "blueprints" for everything that is now or will ever be created in our universe. This field can give us spiritual energy and offers insight into our future lives by showing us what we're being prepped for. It lets us know when something will happen before it does and why it's happening so that we can take the necessary actions to live through those events. Spiritual energy is also required for creating our own reality.

If you want to tap into this energy, you must have aligned your life with the field of Divine Ideas by first and foremost living following those ideas and then doing everything in your power to change any situation or circumstance that is not in alignment with them.

LEARNING FROM YOUR PAST LIVES

Learning from your past lives is a big part of reading the Akashic Records. This is because you can discover what roles in your past life affect your current life and learn from those mistakes instead of making them again. You'll then be able to manifest a better future not just for yourself but for everyone you've affected with your actions in this lifetime as well.

We can explore how we acted and behaved in our past life by reading about it and understanding what we were like. We can then explore why we chose to live such a certain way in that life and how it impacted the world around us. Another benefit of this exploration is finding out why things happen to us in this life when we tend to do something similar to what happened before. Finally, understanding our past lives will help us make better decisions for ourselves in this life because we'll be able to look at other options that are available to us.

CREATING YOUR SANCTUARY

Besides just looking at our past lives, we can also use the Akashic Records to create a sanctuary for ourselves. This sanctuary can consist of anything that will make us feel at ease and relaxed. For example, some people might want to turn their bedroom into a sanctuary by playing tranquil music in the background and decorating it as they please. Other people could choose to create a sanctuary outside by buying a hammock or installing fresh plants around their front yard.

Even if you're not sure what would make you feel more at home when reading the Akashic Records, you'll be presented with an image of what your ideal sanctuary would be like, and this will help you get started on your sanctuary project.

Creating a sanctuary helps you be surrounded by spiritual energy and reminds you of its abundance, opening up your mind to new possibilities. This is why having a sanctuary is so helpful when raising your vibrations. Not only will it inspire you, but it'll help you look at life from another perspective.

EXPERIENCING INNER PEACE

When we experience inner peace, we feel at ease and content. We have a sense of harmony with the universe, and life is filled with meaning. When we're at peace, we can see the world as a beautiful place, and life is more fulfilling. The Akashic Records will help you experience this peace by giving you your insight into your purpose and divine nature. They will help you find your way to inner peace by showing you higher truths and possibilities that were previously hidden from view.

***

Akashic Records are a powerful tool that can help lead you to reach your spiritual goals. With this tool at our disposal, we will understand ourselves better spiritually, manifest more easily into reality, release limiting thoughts or beliefs about self, and create a new world order through conscious living.

The records are an amazing, rich resource for insight and a doorway to tapping into higher realms. An adventure into these records will help you grow spiritually, find healing as well as answers to life's most challenging questions. We must read the Akashic Records responsibly. To do this, we must be in tune with our own energy, know that the process of reading these records is sacred, and take responsibility for what we learn.

Chapter 2. Opening Your Akashic Records and Beginning Your Journey

Everyone has their Akashic Records. This is a knowing of the past, present, and future that creates an individual's destiny and life plan. It is like having your inner GPS available to you at all times. Your Akashic Records are not dependent on what religion you believe in or any spiritual practices you may have engaged in your life. The records exist as pure energy-information systems outside of time and space, and they are available to everyone who knows how to access them! So, let's learn how to open your own Akashic Records and find out more about your life plan and destiny.

If you open your own Akashic Records, you will be able to see specific information about yourself, as well as the life plans of other people. You will also be able to access the answer to any question you have in mind at this moment in time. The Akashic Records are a tool for self-discovery, personal, and spiritual growth.

Open Your Doors

Akashic Records hold all knowledge that ever existed and will ever exist on this planet. Your Record is a compilation of your personal history, including past life experience and each thought and intention you have generated in this lifetime - both good and bad intentions or thoughts.

The Akashic Records exist across a vast space, which is known as the energy continuum. Understanding how to open your doors and connect to this field is a very important skill to master. If you know how to do it, you can use the energy of the Akashic Records as a source for healing yourself and others.

The three main experiences you can have with opening your doors with Akashic Records are the following:

- To Know
- To Heal
- To Spiritual Practices

THE AKASHIC RECORDS FOR KNOWING PURPOSES

Knowing is the act of becoming conscious of what you know and how you know it. You know more than you consciously realize. Your Akashic Records hold a vast amount of information about your past, present, and future experiences.

Knowing is not only about having facts or data. It's also about "knowing" what to do next. Your soul holds its wisdom that connects with the universal consciousness to bring the information you need for your life.

Knowing is a transferable skill outside of your Records. You can use it in your everyday life for personal and professional reasons and the well-being of others.

Knowing is the act of gaining consciousness into what you know and how you know it. Learning how to connect with your Akashic Records through your soul's origin is a process of trust and requires learning to hear your truth.

The Akashic Records are a divine faculty that will not make you dependent on them. They are, in fact, a tool for your divine empowerment. The more you use them, the more strength and clarity you build within yourself to utilize them in healing or any other life purpose.

In many cases, the Records will provide you with a direct answer to your question. You may be given words or images which will speak directly to the issue you asked about, along with verification of its truthfulness. In other situations, you may be shown a symbol such as an object or animal representing an event in your past and causing blockages in your spiritual growth.

Learn about the symbols that you see. Ask your guide or facilitator to tell you anything about them which can help illuminate their meaning to you. I find it helpful to write down what I am being shown so that I won't forget it later on.

Discovering and understanding why these blocks exist will provide insight as to how they can be cleared. For example, if you are shown a symbol of an animal that represents your past life, this may mean that you have carried some of the negative attributes from that life into your current one. This means it is now time to recognize these qualities within yourself and begin to heal them in this lifetime.

The Akashic Records For Healing Purposes

The Akashic Records can be used for healing purposes. The Records hold all knowledge about every illness and its healing so that you can find the best remedy for your physical body and soul as well as to support others in their healing process.

When you tap into the Akashic Records using a trained medium, you are guided by divine intelligence on how to heal yourself or help another person heal. The Akashic Records will guide you to the information you need for whatever health problem is in front of you.

Healing must be approached in a way that looks at all aspects of your life, including your emotional and mental state, as well as any physical disorders that are presenting themselves.

For example, if you have an injury or disease, you must look at your lifestyle to determine what is causing the imbalance. If you have had a string of bad relationships in your life, it's time to rethink why this is happening and how you can change the pattern.

There are many ways to experience this healing. Since each person is different, the healing methods will be unique as well. You may find that you can heal a particular issue by talking about it with someone else who has had similar experiences. In other instances, your body will clear an energy blockage through illness or physical discomfort, such as recurring headaches, nausea, etc.

THE AKASHIC RECORDS FOR SPIRITUAL PRACTICES

The Akashic Records are also used for spiritual purposes, including prayer, meditation, divination, and personal worship. For example, when you pray using the Akashic Records as your divine tool, you can ask to be guided directly by the universe itself.

It's important to note that you are not worshipping the Akashic Records themselves, but rather the universal mind in which they exist - the infinite intelligence of all things.

Using your spiritual practice with your Akashic Records is one way to connect with the universal mind.

The Akashic Records offer a non-denominational and holistic door of access to your spiritual side. You can use it for whatever spiritual practice you need, including worshiping your Divine Being in whatever form they take for you.

You can also use your Akashic Records for divination practices to clarify which course of action you should take in a particular situation.

The Akashic records also aid your practice of meditation. You can clear space within yourself by using the Records' divine energy to increase your self-awareness and transform pain, anger, or grief from past experiences into a vibration that supports any number of positive meditation practices.

The Akashic Records can be used in many ways for different purposes. As you learn how to work within the Records, you will attract information and healing relevant to your life purpose.

In the end, it's about consciousness: being aware of what's happening within yourself or around you at any given moment. You can consider the Records as a tool to support you in being more aware when confusion or a lack of trust arises, which we all experience at different times.

WHO IS YOUR AKASHIC RECORDS GUIDE?

When you learn how to open and use the records, you will find yourself surrounded by a team of Spirit Guides who are available at all times to help you when you ask for assistance.

Your Guide will always be present to support you, but they can only see what's relevant to your life, so not all Guides will work with you consistently.

This is why it's important to focus on the knowledge that comes from within yourself when using the Records - you may need to develop a good relationship with your intuition or inner wisdom to access the Records for yourself fully.

You can contact your Guide when you are ready to start using the Akashic Records, as they will be able to help you begin your journey through them. They may meet you at a specific location within or surrounding the Records, but it's also possible that there isn't any concrete structure involved in your initial contact.

HOW TO ACCESS YOUR RECORDS

Akashic Records are all around you because all things are energy, and the records contain everything that has ever happened, is happening, or will happen. This means that you can access the information contained within them from many different locations. You don't need to travel to a specific place like Stonehenge or the Pyramids in Egypt to get information from your Records. Some people access their Records while they're asleep, others while they're praying, still others when they meditate. There is no one right way to go about it.

Your records are available at any time, and you'll be able to connect to them using your intuition and inner wisdom.

You can access your Records consciously by taking time out of your busy schedule once a day to sit quietly with yourself, or you can access the Records while you're sleeping. If this interests you, I suggest trying it both ways and see what works best for you based on how you can feel more connected to your Records. From my experience, meditating as part of my spiritual practice is the best way for me to access information from the Records, but it could be different for you, and that's okay.

Opening your Akashic Records is a powerful way to heal and grow. But you must learn how to work within them for this process to be fruitful. Your Guide will help teach you more about the Records and what information they contain from any place at any time. Spiritual practices like meditation are an excellent tool for opening up communication with your Guides and learning how best to access your Akashic Records.

To open your Akashic Records, you need the following:

AGREEMENTS

Agreements are a series of statements that guide and define when and how the Akashic Records are opened. They help you understand what you are seeing, feeling, and experiencing as it pertains to the Records. Agreements explain what is happening when you are in these altered states of consciousness, and they offer direction to ensure that your experience remains safe for yourself and others around you.

Agreements give structure within the Records so that you can react appropriately to the information that is given to you from them. They ensure that what you see, hear, and feel during your journey through the Records is relevant without causing you stress or trauma.

Agreements help you learn how to focus on healing yourself instead of turning your attention toward others who are in need of assistance. This aspect of healing within the Akashic Records is crucial to your capacity for self-healing.

Agreements allow you to work with other people while keeping your healing a private matter between you, your Records, and your Guide. You can have relationships with others while still maintaining the integrity of the information that comes to you from within your Records and keeps your Guides anonymous.

VISUALIZATION

Visualization is a basic set of instructions that visually guides you to the Akashic Records' entrance. It creates a safe place to visit from which you can approach the Records. From this point, you can learn more about your Guides and request that they begin working with you in other types of healing meditations or healing sessions.

Visualization is also required to enter the Akashic Records because it creates an environment in which your Guides can enter into the Records with you to explore the information that comes forward in a safe way for both of you.

Visualization helps you feel relaxed and centered before opening your Records. If you are anxious or excited, it will be hard for your Guides to help you find what they need to guide you into healing yourself. Visualization ensures that you are centered before moving into the Records.

Visualization helps create an atmosphere within which your Guides can prepare and program new information about how to heal yourself through your Records. Visualization puts all of the necessary pieces in place before you ask your Guides to start working with you.

Visualization is a specific action that takes time and patience to master. You must be willing to sit with things for a while before learning how to enter your Records seamlessly.

Visualization is also an excellent tool for anchoring a given memory or healing session so that upon your return from the journey within the Records, you have something physical that will help remind you of what has happened.

Visualization allows you to focus in a specific way that communicates to your Guides that you are ready for them to begin working with you.

BLESSING

Blessing is words of intention for your Akashic Records entry and experience. They are specific words spoken from the heart to set the stage for your Record journey.

When you bless an area or object, you create a field of energy used to guide and protect what is called into your awareness. Blessing prepares your Records for the work ahead with them by offering protection and guidance so that they can be more effective as a healing method for you. The blessing will help ensure that the information that comes into your consciousness during your Record journey is related only to healing in some way and not scattered all over the place.

Taking time to bless what is about to happen opens you energetically so that you can begin to receive healing guidance from within the Akashic Records. Blessing helps to focus your attention to have an immediate sense of calm and peace, which helps you feel less fear regarding the journey ahead.

Using formal wording for entering into the Akashic Records will ensure that you maintain a sense of safety and trust in what is about to happen. It also provides direction, protection, and security for information in the Records that might otherwise come forward as scattered or unrelated thoughts.

Blessing also helps you to be energetic, calm, and centered before you enter into your Records. Blessing opens you to receiving the guidance of a healing nature during your Record journey so that it is easier for you to know what kind of healing you need.

Blessing helps you release your expectations regarding your Akashic Records journey and sets the stage for clear thinking once you are in the experience. It also helps protect your Records from absorbing any negative energy that might accidentally be brought into the healing environment by attaching itself onto an individual who is present with you when you are in the Records.

PROCESS

The process for opening your Akashic Records is based on your agreements, the method you use, combining visualization and blessing. The process begins with an opening statement to release any expectations that you may have. Once that is completed, the second part of the process involves a request for open Records followed by an attunement for healing communication between you and your Guides before entering your Records.

You must be willing to let go of expectations to experience opening your Records fully. You must also be willing to trust what happens when you work with the Records. Trust and letting go to enable you to allow guidance from within your Records to come into your consciousness without interference from what is taking place around you.

***

Opening your Records requires you to have a relaxed state of body, mind, and spirit when working with them. You cannot force yourself into an agreement or use negative thinking to breach them. In fact, you cannot open your Records if there is a negative thought in your mind at the time you try to do so. You must be willing to let go of thoughts that may arise and trust that they are being cared for by your Guides while you work with both of them in unison through an attunement for communication.

Opening your Records requires you to have an ability to focus and a desire to enter into the experience. It is necessary for you to feel emotionally stable, grounded within yourself energetically, and clear with intent before entering into the open Records method. Do not use opening the Records when you are tired or for a specific reason. Simply enter into the Records when you feel good, as this allows your Guides to work with you in a better way and enables you to be clear for information within them.

CHAPTER 3. ACCESSING YOUR AKASHIC RECORDS: DOS AND DON'TS

Akashic Records are the traces of all that has ever happened in the universe. The Akashic Records are like a huge library containing every event, thought, and feeling ever since the beginning of time. The Records contain the history of every soul, including our thoughts and feelings on any subject; each thought or feeling is stored permanently in the form of energy.

Every person's Akashic Records can be accessed by them at any time to view their personal history and experience. But remember these ground rules, as there are some definite dos and don'ts in connecting with your Akashic Records.

NO ONE CAN ACCESS YOUR AKASHIC RECORDS WITHOUT YOUR EXPLICIT CONSENT.

If you do not wish to view a particular segment of your Akashic Records for any reason, it will be closed off to all readers until the time comes that you are ready to see this portion of yourself. It may be difficult or impossible for readers to access your Records if something in your energy field does not want them to read a part of it. However, once this energy has been neutralized, that portion will be opened in your Akashic Record for all to see.

SOMEONE WHO KNOWS HOW TO OPEN AKASHIC RECORDS CAN ACCESS YOURS, OR YOU CAN LEARN TO OPEN YOUR OWN.

No one may throw out information from your Akashic Records. If you do not want certain information revealed, then the owner of that energy will have to deal with it himself. People often do not remember why they had a certain feeling or thought at a particular point in their lives, but it will be obvious when they see the Record for themselves.

You should be very careful about what goes into your energy field (your thought patterns), as the next reader of your Akashic Records may not be as aware of this type of projection as you are. Keep in mind that others will read your Records, and if they do not understand what has been imprinted there, they may try to "correct" the impression left on your energy field.

It would be best if you learned how to prevent other people from entering your Akashic Records. As the owner of your energy, you have a right to make sure that only YOU read it and that others do not try to change what is there. If someone else does try to enter your Akashic Records, they must first ask permission from YOUR energy or wait until you allow them entrance.

ADULTS AGED 18 YEARS AND OVER ARE ALLOWED ACCESS TO THE AKASHIC RECORDS.

Children have not had enough experience in life to bear what they may find on their Records. Parents, when your children reach the age of 18, then this information should be given to them.

A child's Akashic Records will automatically be sealed until they are adults and ready for whatever knowledge it holds. If a child has died before this age, then their Akashic Records will be sealed as well.

Psychics and mediums may not reveal information from the Records to others outside of their profession without your permission. Do not allow psychics or fortunetellers to "read" your Akashic Record unless you have checked their references and you are certain of the work they do.

If you choose to use a psychic or medium, make sure that this person is trained to work with the Akashic Records and provide a certification of their credentials.

WITHIN THE AKASHIC RECORDS, CONFIDENTIALITY IS NEEDED AND IRREVERSIBLE.

All information within the Akashic Records must be kept hidden from everyone, including your closest friends.

No one outside of a professional reader of the Records may know anything about what is in that person's Record, except the owner. However, if you have shared intimate details with a person who has since passed on, you may be surprised to find them telling someone else in the Records.

This is not the fault of the Akashic Record reader; it is a natural phenomenon and one which you need to be aware of if you share intimate personal details with anyone other than yourself or your Professional Reader (a trained, professional Akashic reader who has a certificate of credentials).

There are some secrets that you may not be comfortable having revealed even to your psychic or medium. It is always the owner's choice whether or not he wishes to make something confidential within his Record. A Professional Reader can only reveal information on the "outer" levels of information in an unopened Record but cannot know anything about the "inner" levels of information without the permission of the owner or court order.

THE QUESTIONS AND ISSUES HIGHLIGHTED BY THE PERSON WHOSE AKASHIC RECORDS HAVE BEEN OPENED ARE ADDRESSED IN AN AKASHIC RECORD READING.

Information may be revealed within the Akashic Records, but only issues and questions relevant to the person who has had their Record opened will be addressed.

The Akashic Records should not be opened for entertainment purposes.

Akashic Record readings are never done as part of a "group reading." Each individual must have an opportunity to ask their questions and receive answers accordingly.

A Professional Reader can access Akashic Records for educational purposes, but only AFTER the owner of that particular Record has been permitted to do so. The Akashic Records are not intended for others' curiosity!

The rules governing information in the Akashic Records are the same rules that govern private conversations within a person's home. If you do not want others to overhear what you are saying, then keep your voice down!

Conversations in the Akashic Records that should be kept private include:
- Personal information concerning other people; secrets; intimate details of one's personal life.
- Knowledge of Akashic Records is not to be shared with others.
- Business information; knowledge that could damage other people's careers; or secrets of any kind to which you were privy in your lifetime.
- Information about crimes - especially violent crimes and murders - should be kept hidden within the Akashic Records if you have been a witness to that crime.

Information may be revealed within the Records about events that you were involved in but which was not relevant at your time; information that it is now time to reveal should be discussed with your Professional Reader before this can occur.

YOUR QUESTIONS ARE THE BASIS FOR AN AKASHIC RECORD READING.

The Professional Reader may sometimes throw out a question, but the Akashic Records will always respond to your questions first.

Akashic Record readings help you focus on the most important issues in your life at this time.

While some information within the Akashic Records can be "life-changing," it is not meant to take the place of your intuition.

There is no need to ask questions that you already know the answers to.

Akashic Records are not created for teaching history. They deal with events in the present and future, as they affect people living today.

It is a waste of time to ask about things that happened in the past; you can always search for that information yourself.

Akashic Record readings are not based upon astrology, numerology, or any other esoterica (e.g., tarot cards). These disciplines may enhance your understanding and enable you to interpret what goes on during an Akashic Records reading. Still, they should not be used for the basis of information in a reading.

Akashic Record readings are always given concerning the person whose Records have been opened.

The Akashic Records will reveal only what we need or want to know; no more and no less! They do NOT give out all the knowledge in the universe but only what is relevant to us at this point.

A Professional Reader must be a "non-judgmental" person; they will not judge the person whose Records have been opened - and who, therefore, may receive information that they do not want to hear.

YOUR LEGAL NAME IS IMPORTANT.

Names are very important identifiers in the Akashic Records. People who are "known" in their lifetimes will often have information about them revealed within the Akashic Records, but only if that person is of "public interest" during their lifetime.

People who make a difference in their community have information available about them within their Akashic Record. People who are famous, infamous, or notorious will need to be clarified before opening their Records.

Always use your legal name when opening your Records. Do not use your "nicknames" or your middle name(s). People who are searching for information about themselves using their legal names will find their Akashic Records without any problems.

MIND-ALTERING SUBSTANCES, SUCH AS DRUGS AND ALCOHOL, CAN IMPEDE YOU.

Drugs and alcohol distort your perception of reality. It may not be clear - either to you or the Professional Reader - if your sense of reality is distorted. This can cause errors in an Akashic Records Reading. Opening your Akashic Records in this state is disrespectful to your Spirit Guides and an insult to the Akashic Records. It is best not to open them at all. If you must do so, please wait until later or have a friend read for you with no drugs or alcohol in your system. Prescription meds for your physical health do not affect the results of an Akashic Records reading.

MIXING RITUALS ISN'T THE BEST APPROACH.

Opening your Akashic Records should not be integrated with other rituals you also practice. Akashic Records readings are a personal experience. When other spiritual rituals and practices are combined, it can make the insights confusing for you and even your Professional Reader.

AKASHIC RECORD READINGS DO NOT REPLACE THERAPY OR REMEDY A SITUATION.

The information revealed in an Akashic Records reading will not be enough to "fix" a situation or help to solve a problem for you. You must deal with these situations and problems using all of the available tools, including therapy. Problems are often generated when people think that opening their Records will be a shortcut to solving their issues. It is not.

Don't ask what's going to happen in the future.

The general rule is that the Akashic Records are not used to predict future events. It is rare for information of this sort to be revealed in an Akashic Record reading. If such information is revealed, it is never complete nor exact. No one's life can ever be broken down into neat sequences of time. Our future will always be affected by the choices we make, and those around us. The Akashic Records are the history of our life energy - they are not a crystal ball.

When reading the Records, it's critical to immerse yourself in the experience.

It would be best if you spent enough time with your Records to get the best results. Reading a few pages or skimming through them will probably not provide you with any "aha!" moments. You should allow yourself some quiet time to relax and read and look at things in your Records - as if you were reading a book you've been wanting to read for a long time.

The Entities And Their Roles In The Akashic Realm

There are beings that you will encounter when you open your Akashic Record. They perform specific roles in the Akashic Realm, and some will assist you personally. These entities responsible for "writing" or recording your life story will help you tap into the information of your Record. Other guides and energy beings in that realm affect how you view that information once it appears before you.

Most of these entities are not strangers to you. In fact, they may be very familiar friends and family members in your everyday existence.

As you tap into your Akashic Record, it is helpful to know the names of some of those beings that assist you on this journey.

The Divine Creator created our universe and all life forms within it.

The Lords of the Records are huge beings that surround your Guardian Entity. They do not interfere in anything that is going on with your life, but they are there as a backup and to help protect you. They can also be called upon when needed by someone who has made contact with the Akashic Realm.

The Guardian Entity watches over your Akashic Records. It will answer any of your questions and show you exactly what you need to see when using your Akashic Record.

The Being of Light is the one who will actually be showing you actual memories and experiences from your past lives. It will have its own personality, so try not to direct it too much but let it do what it does best - show things in an orderly fashion.

Your Blue Ray Master is there to help you understand any information that may be too difficult or complex for you to understand. It will also translate, in words, anything the Being of Light shows you during your session.

The Ascended Masters are there as a support group just in case anything goes wrong with your session, and they can give you a little bit of their own energy if needed. These are Ascended Masters from different traditions, including Christianity, Islam, Buddhism, and many more.

The Group Soul from the Pleiades are masters of energy and information. This is why they are assigned to translate what you see and hear into a form that you can understand. Otherwise, it would be too confusing because nobody speaks in riddles when viewing their Akashic Records.

Your Higher Self is your own higher soul. It is your connection with the Divine Creator, and it will come to you when you make contact with the Akashic Records to show that you are in touch with your own Divine Essence.

Your Other Lives Guidance Team includes all of those who have worked together in previous lives to help each other evolve into their greatest potential. They will also be there to help you understand the many nuances of your Akashic Record that may otherwise be too difficult for you to grasp.

You can call upon any or all of these entities when making contact with your own personal Akashic Records, as they are indeed members of your Soul Family.

Good preparation will enhance the experience of accessing your Records and help you get information relevant to you today. Remember, when you access your Records, whatever is contained within them will be awakened for the accessed period. The more you are in the energy of love, peace, and joy, the more you will consciously experience a stress-free life. If you wish to access your Records, it is important that you feel good about yourself and do not have any negative feelings or experiences about yourself.

To access this information, you must first open your Akashic Records by connecting with your Higher Self. After opening up to higher guidance, it is possible to access any person's Akashic Records or any historical event simply by asking for it. There are three steps involved in accessing these Records:
1) Connecting with Spirit
2) Opening Your Own Akashic Record
3) Accessing Another Person's Akashic Record

The process begins by connecting with the spirit through meditation, prayer, and other spiritual practices so that you can receive guidance from your higher self. You can also open the Records through intense visualization and intention by imagining a bright light in your third eye area, representing your connection with spirit.

The next step is to ask your higher self if it is possible to access any historical information on a specific person or event. If yes, you must state what you want to know and then ask if you can have permission. You may even be given a date that is of importance as this relates to the time when the information was imprinted into the Akashic Records, or you may be told that no such record exists yet because the information has not been released by either yourself through collective consciousness or from spirit in the form of a dream or prophecy.

When it is time to access another person's Akashic Records, you must first ask your higher self if it is possible. Often the request will involve that you have permission from the individual in question before accessing this information. It is also possible that they have not yet asked spirit for permission to access their Akashic Records since they may not be ready to face the information within them.

Once you have received permission by either yourself or from the person in question, then ask your higher self for a date of birth, name, place of birth, and any other relevant details about that individual. You may also be shown symbols and colors, which will help you access the right Akashic Records. The symbols and colors will be different for each person, so you need to know what they should look like when connecting with your higher self.

When opening up another person's Akashic Records, it may feel odd as this is an unaccustomed way of thinking and perceiving, but it is only your ego that will be concerned about this and not your higher self. Once you have experienced the information for yourself, it will help to raise your level of consciousness. It is important to remember that when you are accessing another person's Akashic Records, then they are always present but in a way that feels more powerful than in your normal waking state of consciousness.

***

There are some basic guidelines that you need to follow when accessing the Akashic Records. Firstly, it is important to remember that you cannot change anything once you have seen something by accessing a person's Akashic Records. Hence, it is best not to ask or look for things that could be personally hurtful or damaging. For example, you should not ask to see a person's future if you know that it will be bad for them somehow. It is best not to access another person's Akashic Records unless permitted since your higher self may give you information without their knowledge, leading to problems later on in the relationship.

Also, remember not to access the Akashic Records of children or newborn babies since they have not yet experienced enough life to form meaningful connections with their actions. Therefore, it would be an invasion of privacy. It is also important not to ask questions about others without permission. The information you receive from your higher self will always be true, but there may be a slightly distorted version of it for the sake of your learning, so check before you proceed.

Finally, bear in mind that when connecting with the Akashic Records, there is always an energetic presence of both yourself and another person involved, even though they are not physically present at the time. It is also possible to access other people's Akashic Records in the future after gaining experience and ability, although this comes with a warning. If you access someone's Akashic Records too often, you may alter their destiny since they create it themselves through free will.

You have now gained an insight into how to access information within the Akashic Record safely, so I urge you never to be afraid of what you might find since it will only serve to enlighten you.

.

CHAPTER 4. CONNECTING WITH YOUR INNER CONSCIOUSNESS THROUGH THE ETERNAL TIMELINE

Akasha is where thoughts, actions, and feelings reside when they are not actively being expressed. Past, present, and future records are connected to the spirit of our consciousness, which is called the Eternal Timeline of the Akashic Records.

A special system of symbols and geometric forms has been designed to organize the information so that it means something only if you understand it as an individual. In other words, this pattern is understandable only to your consciousness.

Thus, if we find a way to connect our consciousness with Akasha, it means that our spirit can be connected to unlimited knowledge about time and space.

PAST RECORDS

Past Records are events that have happened and materialized within the Akashic Records. These records exist in two forms. The first form defines memory as an event, reaction, or feeling stored in the Akasha. The second form designates the act of recalling to mind thoughts, feelings, or memories from previous events. Within the Akashic Records, human beings can connect with their past in many different ways. There are many ways you can get Past Records, and some of them include symbols, geometric patterns, and geometry principles. You might also access your Past Records by connecting to your spirit, as humans have limited knowledge about time and space.

Past Records also include deja vus. A deja vu is a French term that means "already seen." Most people will experience deja vu at some time in their lives, and it is considered to be very common. It could be as simple as thinking something you've never seen before looks familiar or seeing an unusual combination of numbers and thinking you've seen it before. Some people experience deja vu regularly.

Past Records also include premonitions, dreams, or visions. A premonition is a feeling or impression that something specific will happen in the future sense as an individual will have about past or future events through Akashic Records. Most people sometimes get this kind of feeling, but they ignore it.

It is often the case that people choose to be reincarnated because they want new opportunities in their next life. Often, these reasons are related to making up for mistakes or patterns from previous lives; others may wish for a better quality of life than what has been experienced before. Still, more would like the opportunity to present themselves this time around. Regardless of why you might desire to incarnate again, there's no doubt that past life memories can affect your current one - through karma records that hold all experiences and emotions attained during each lifetime that was lived.

Karma encompasses thoughts, words, and actions that are considered to have a specific impact on future events. Simply put, karma governs how we treat others as well as ourselves - each of our actions produces energy stored in the Akashic Records; this energy affects other people and us over time. Over time, your karma begins to take on a specific form - it shapes you in every moment.

The key is to remember that we truly can change our karma; this can be done in many ways. We're often given signs and omens every day, letting us know if we need to alter our actions, words, and feelings. Our past lives can also influence our present ones. The easiest way to access this information is through symbols - little reminders of what we need to know to release any negativity from previous lifetimes.

Each symbol holds a wealth of knowledge about a specific lifetime and how karma might have been created; for example, an eagle represents freedom, but it might also represent the death of a loved one or a personal struggle that is endured. Every symbol has multiple and different meanings depending on how you approach them; for this reason, it's really important to pull back and look at your life from outside yourself - don't get too focused on your point of view because it may have become slightly distorted over time.

The best way to do this is through meditation so that you can open up your soul and receive messages from the Akashic Records - all a part of your Eternal Timeline with infinite knowledge about time and space.

Past Records also include behaviors, activities, and thoughts throughout our day-to-day lives. Obviously, if you're in a bad mood and treat people poorly, this information will be stored in the Akashic Records. Not only will this affect you from this point forward, but it'll also affect those around you as well.

How often do you think about your past lives? Do you think they're connected to your present life in some ways? Do you think they will have an impact on your future? If so, what kind of influence do you think it has or will have? What if you don't remember anything from a previous life? Think about this for a moment.

PRESENT RECORDS

In contrast, Present Records are the events that are presently occurring within our lives. These records exist in many ways. One way is when you tell someone about an event that still happened in your life, and they say, "I know." This type of record will be recorded within Akasha's symbols and geometric forms to classify memories according to their type. Another way is to have feelings and thoughts that come up before having a particular experience or event happen. These records will also be classified according to their type regarding their relevance to the present through the Akashic Records system of symbols and geometric forms.

Think about how a symbol in the form of an emoticon is like Present Records because it signifies our feelings and thoughts at that moment. When you're at a point in your life where you've been feeling down and nervous, people around you may be sending out signals or signs for you to pay attention to and listen to. These will be stored as Present Records so long as we access the information before going to make right on these events.

Every time a thought, word, or feeling is expressed, it becomes a part of your Present Records - if you tell someone that you're going to do something but then don't follow through with what you've said, this will be recorded as well. Our thoughts and feelings are always being recorded in the Akashic Records because they exist in the Eternal Timeline.

Anything that is done to others or for others will also be recorded in the Present Records, even if we don't know it at the time. One way this can happen is when you do something nice for someone else, but they don't appreciate your efforts; still, the thoughts and feelings of appreciation will be recorded in the Present Records for them to have at a later time when they remember what you've done.

The upbringing of children will also be recorded within your Present Records because they are being affected by life daily. Suppose your child is constantly exposed to violence or poor behavior. In that case, these records will show this kind of activity, particularly when they are participating in behavior they know isn't right.

Another way these records will be shown is through our health. We can easily see how poor eating habits or lack of exercise could be recorded in the Akashic Records and affect us later on when it comes to illness. The same goes for any medication that has been taken, herbal remedies, etc. These records will be stored in the Present Records to remember later when you are no longer sick or need any medication.

When we think about all of the activities that we engage in daily, it is amazing how many things are recorded - whether or not we want them to be or not! And those events that you think aren't being recorded, there are always symbols and geometric forms to prove otherwise.

If these records are so important, why don't we remember them? Because this is not the purpose of Present Records. It's not their intent to remind us where they came from or whose thoughts they were, but rather to be the moment captured in time.

It would be pretty hard to remember the experiences and events in every detail. For example, if you were having thoughts about taking a particular action or making a decision based on something that happened to you - like "that's not what I want for me at this moment." Then, later on down the road, when it comes to fruition, you'll have the thought, "that's not what I wanted for me."

This is your opportunity to re-access or record a new event. There are so many different kinds of records that these symbols will be classified according to their purpose and meaning. For instance, if someone thinks about taking revenge on another person, they can go to the Akashic Records and put this negative symbol into a positive symbol. Then they can release it back into the universe to help create something good for them instead of bad.

FUTURE RECORDS

Future Records are events or actions that have not yet happened but will happen in the future. In this way, we can see our entire life as a set of records. Since the future is not determined, it can be seen as limitless possibilities that could happen anytime and in any place. Therefore, we must consider the effects of everything we do and think in the present moment. Everything you learn from past events will help you make better decisions about handling future events.

Most importantly, we must understand that these records are never-ending - they go on forever. In this way, there are no mistakes in life. Every event in our lives is for a reason, and every thought we have is significant. Suppose an event does not happen the way we anticipated. In that case, this can be changed through self-inquiry or going within to access the Eternal Timeline of the Akashic Records, which reveals all possibilities that could happen. The Akashic Records will give you the tools necessary to create a better future for yourself or your child.

It is important to realize that these records exist within all of us. They are not just limited to one person's life, but rather they encompass everything in existence. The significance of this should prompt everyone to go inward and ask, how does this affect me? How does this record apply to me now?

Know that there are no mistakes in life, only lessons. Everything happens for a reason, and every event has some significance in your present or future. In this way, you can begin to see how important it is to take the time to understand what is happening around you, rather than being so busy with your life all of the time.

What are you going to do today to change something in your future? What lesson has already been learned? How will this event affect my greater growth and understanding through a different perspective or new self-awareness? If you're not taking full control over your thoughts, words, and actions, your future will not be what you want it to be. But if you're willing to take full responsibility for how you handle every moment of life, then the possibilities are endless.

What can I do now to create a better future? How can I start creating my desired outcomes right here and now? What relationship am I in that will make my future better if I change or improve it now?

These are the kinds of questions you must ask yourself every day to help create a new positive reality for yourself. It is important to remember that everything you do in your life creates a new record that affects who you become. If this does not fit with what you want, it is time to take responsibility for your life and become the author of your own experience.

From this place of awareness, everything becomes possible. You can create new records that will help produce what you want in your future with the people around you. In this way, one record can affect another, which creates an infinite timeline of possibilities.

The Akashic Records show you how to control your life and understand where you are in the Eternal Timeline of existence. It is a formless process, and it will help anyone who seeks more information about their purpose on Earth to become a master over creation. There is only one creator but many variables: anything and everything is possible.

Step 1. It's important to know that any thought, feeling, or action exists as a record in the Akashic Records. This has been proven through years of experiments with individuals who have gone deep within themselves to get answers from the Records.

Step 2. Now it is time for you to use the Akashic Records within yourself. This will help you get rid of all the unconscious programs and records that don't serve you, and it may invite new characters or situations into your life.

Step 3. The next step is to fully utilize this information to create a better future for what you want by making new records that work for you. This will help you to create new possibilities in your life by focusing on the future rather than dwelling in regret about the past.

Step 4. Now it is time to connect with the Eternal Timeline and then open portals into that timeline. Once you have left a mark on this record or solidified a connection with it, you will have a new feeling of knowing in your life. You may also see that some events from the past were meant to happen based on what happened afterward.

Step 5. The last step is to find new ways of thinking about yourself and the world around you – by connecting all the records within your Akashic Records. This will help you to experience the world differently based on what records are interacting with each other.

It is important for you to recognize that this is an ongoing process, not a one-time thing. It takes practice and dedication for it to work truly. The universe works through full-circle cycles, and you must be back in balance with yourself before you can continue to move ahead.

***

As you can see, connecting with your inner consciousness through the Eternal Timeline of the Akashic Records is a process that will help people create better records for their future. It's important to take responsibility for one's life and become the author of one's experience to make new possibilities happen. In this way, it takes practice and dedication for things to work.

.

CHAPTER 5. THE POWER OF PAST LIVES: EXPLORING THROUGH THE AKASHIC RECORDS

The Akashic Records are the all-encompassing records of every thought, word, and deed that has ever occurred on Earth. They contain information about your past lives as well as what may be happening in your future. You can access this information through your divine inner wisdom, and it is from the Akashic Records that our guides can pull the information they give us in readings.

The Akashic Records can offer clarity around your life path, your purpose, and how to move forward. The Akashic Records act as a repository of all knowledge, and the belief that human souls never truly die means you can use it to learn about your past lives. The idea of past lives may seem strange, but it speaks to our identity and the notion that we are eternal beings. It is from this knowing that we have the power to transform our lives.

PAST LIVES AND THE AKASHIC RECORDS

Past lives are an important aspect of the Akashic Records. Most believe that these past lives greatly impact how one lives their current life, including relationships and attracting certain futures. Accessing one's past lives through the Akashic Records will allow one to learn about what may be happening in the future. This gives you a tremendous amount of control over the kind of future you attract, since learning about who you were in previous lives and how your actions created certain fates for yourself makes it easier to see what may be happening in this life. Past life regression is very powerful when exploring the Akashic Records because it allows one to better understand themselves. Akasha is not the realm of only remembering your past lives but also a place to access future information.

If you are living out the many lifetimes described in your Akashic Records, and there is an ebb and flow to your soul's experience - a sense that you have deep roots going back eons, then why in the world would you limit yourself to living only one lifetime at a time? Why not tap into all that your soul has been through by exploring your past lives? The Akashic Records are such a powerful way of tapping into your soul's experience. Accessing them is where our souls truly shine.

The human spirit incarnates into a new life, carrying the accumulated experiences and knowledge from past lives. We may not remember these previous lives as they were lived in this current lifetime, yet we are guided by something inside us that can help us gain access to our Akashic Records. To see our purpose for being on Earth right now and our destiny, we need to tune into the deepest part of ourselves by tapping into past life experiences.

Whether you agree with reincarnation or not, it's a concept that has been around for centuries and continues to be relevant. Since reincarnation is an eternally persistent idea, one needs to ask why it has such staying power. The theory of rebirth seems too intuitive for people to have not been thinking about it since the beginning of time. In most cultures throughout history, some accounts relate to elements of this metaphysical ideology. The most important thing about this whole discussion is how you feel about it. Looking at it from only one perspective - either believing or not believing - will block you from getting the most out of exploring the Akashic Records.

The concept that our souls do not die and reincarnate into other lifetimes is nothing new. This idea has been around for thousands of years, especially in Eastern philosophy and religion. It would be impossible to discuss this subject without mentioning how it ties into the Akashic Records since reincarnation is one of the most important components of this phenomenon. Everything that we think, feel, and do in our lives gets recorded into Akashic Records. Every word, thought, or action will get stored away. This is information on a much deeper level than what can be charted through time, it's about us as souls - our personalities, emotions and experiences - on an even deeper level than time itself.

EVERYONE HAVE PAST LIVES

Past lives have been proven to be true through cognitive or emotional recall. The subtle energy of the human body can be monitored, and this will provide evidence for past life memories. The subtle body is also said to provide energy for us, which is an important part of living. This energy helps us to carry out activities that are required in our current life.

True believers in past lives may believe that past-life therapy can help with phobias, addiction problems, and even health issues. For the most part, people who are addicted may not enjoy their current life because they do not particularly like what their current life entails. Also, some people may feel as if they are being punished when they have a health issue such as cancer; however, as mentioned before, this could result from something that happened to them in a previous life. No matter what you believe, making personal changes in your current life can help you feel better and bring positivity into your life.

AKASHIC PAST LIFE READINGS

It is believed that past lives play a role in Akashic Record readings. This is because the Akashic Records contain the records of every thought, feeling and action we have ever had. Past-life readings are a type of Akashic Records session where you can access your akashic past life data. This is guided by questions that you have about your past lifetimes. These readings vary from person to person, with some people being told about their past lives and what they were like while others don't recall anything. One example of this is a gentleman who believed he was an Egyptian slave, only to find out he was the same age as when he died and even wearing the same clothes he was when the building he was working on collapsed.

Another example would be a woman who had hot flashes and felt like she was going through a menopause-type state even though she was very young. In her past life, she had been murdered while taking a bath, which is why this emotion was coming back to her. In this case, it is understandable how the memory could have led to a belief that she would die young because of her experiences in another life.

This gentleman and woman could recall specific memories about their past lives, which can provide you with a better understanding of how Akashic Records work. They acquired knowledge based on their actions and thoughts in past lifetimes. Past-life readings are an effective way to learn about the self because they can provide you with more insight than just asking your next step. Knowledge of the true meaning and purpose of your life may be revealed through this type of reading.

When you're looking for answers that don't exist in your current life, why particular concerns are holding you back or identifying patterns in your relationships with your loved ones, reaching out to your previous lives can be quite helpful. You can choose to visit Your Most Recent Past Life, Your Most Significant Past Life, or Your Soul's Past life of Choice.

REGRESSION VERSUS READING OF PAST LIFE MEMORIES

One of the differences between regression and reading of Akashic Records is their accessibility. When looking for information about one's past life through regression, it is done through hypnotherapy or past-life regression techniques, such as age progression. It may take some time before one can recall all the information they need from their past lives. However, in an Akashic Records reading, you will instantly have access to your memories from previous lifetimes without having to go through this process.

Another difference between regression and reading is the accuracy of information obtained by each method. With regression, there is no guarantee that the memories are accurate or true. For instance, if someone were to regress into a past life of an Australian Aborigine who was a shaman, the person could be convinced that they are actually from this lifetime. On the other hand, if you use the Akashic Records, it is believed to be direct truth about your past lives without any speculation involved due to their authenticity.

The aim of both techniques is similar: to provide information about one's past life and how it pertains to the present. However, the Akashic Records can provide you with a greater number of details in less time.

KARMA AND AKASHIC RECORDS

Akasha is a Sanskrit word that is translated as "space" or "ether." Akasha is often associated with the Hindu belief of karma. Karma in this context represents the sum of one's actions which in turn determine future situations in life, as well as the only form of true justice since it deals with both intent and deed.

Since karma encompasses both bodily and mental action, it inevitably includes Akashic Records, which are fragments of memory from past lives. Thus, although karma focuses on actions within one lifetime, it also carries over into future lifetimes due to memories from previous lives being stored in our Akashic Records.

People who believe in the existence of the Akashic Records also believe that karma is a form of inevitable cause and effect. The belief is that when one consciously works to purify their present life, it increases knowledge and spiritual growth. However, some claim that this can be done through observation without intentionally changing one's actions.

If you learn of your karma and Akashic Records, it can help you realize what situations will likely occur in the future. You might feel as if you're living in the wrong period or suffering by being at the wrong place at the wrong time. Akasha is a complex concept; thus, there are no clear answers to exactly explain the Akashic Records. However, it is important for you to understand that those who believe in karma also adhere to the idea of Akashic Records and their collection.

WHAT DETAILS SHOULD YOU CHECK IN PAST LIVES?

One of the major details to note in your past lives is how you interacted with your surroundings. Did you feel happy and content or perhaps tormented? Were your actions good or bad? What was your emotional state like? The more you can recall what happened during this time, the better understanding you will have of where these memories may have originated.

Another way to get a better idea of what your past life was like is by looking at the people in the lives that surrounded you. For instance, if you were surrounded by people who were thriving financially, it might be a sign that this lifetime should be spent making money to get out of poverty. Likewise, being near people in an abusive situation may suggest that this lifetime should be spent learning about self-defense.

Different things to note are dreams, visions, and feelings you have while in a past life state. You can also include the emotions of others who surround you. It tells you more information about how your current situations are affecting the lives around you and which direction is acting as a catalyst for your karma. If you find that someone is in danger or feeling down, it might be because of something you did in the past. Thus, you can work hard to make improvements.

THE QUALITY OF YOUR PRESENT LIFE AS ONE OF YOUR PAST LIVES

So, you're curious about how your present life will fare in the Akashic Records? Reading an account of what you did in a past life can help change your perspective on what you're doing. If you don't like how your present life is turning out, then it may be time to start making changes. The best way to make these changes is by shifting from one state of mind into another, and this can be done through reading about your account from a past life. It can help you to understand why your present life hasn't turned out the way you wanted, or it can steer you in a positive direction.

A good approach to this would be making a list of things that need improvement. After reading about how they were handled in the past, you might find yourself changing some of your behaviors. If there is something that you need to work harder on, then it may be time to get into practice. On the other hand, if you are doing better than before, maybe you've been in this situation before. If this is the case, what can you learn from your past life and how does it offer a solution for your present life?

As you learn more about what kind of karma and past lives you have, it can help to improve the quality of your life. If there are things that need improvement, perhaps it's time to change yourself or adjust your behavior to avoid negatively attracting karma. Likewise, if something needs correction, then maybe it's a sign that you should change your ways.

If you change some of your behaviors and replace irrational beliefs with rational ones, it may positively impact your future. If you do not change your ways and continue to hold on to irrationalities, it may impact other parts of your life as well.

The quality of your present life is relative to the decisions you make. The more you learn about what karma may be lurking around in your past, the less likely you are to make irrational or wrong choices. By making yourself aware of what happened in a previous life, then perhaps will help you to understand why certain things are occurring.

***

The Akashic Records are believed to have a huge impact on the way we live our lives, our relationships, and the kind of future we attract. Those who believe in accessing them think that they can reveal information about one's past lives, allowing those who access their Records more control over their fate depending on what type of life they are currently living. Some people claim to see specific events from another person's past or even an entire lifetime through these Records. With so much power at your fingertips for such little effort, it is understandable why some might want to explore this possibility further.

CHAPTER 6. SEEING THROUGH THE LENS OF YOUR PAST AND PRESENT LIVES IN THE AKASHIC RECORDS

There are many ways to find your purpose in life. One of the most popular is through Akashic Records, a record of every event that has ever happened on Earth and in Heaven. The Akashic Records contain all the knowledge you could imagine because they're not restricted by time or space like we are here on Earth.

People can ask questions about their lives and receive answers from their Higher Self through opening their Akashic Records. The Akashic Records are an incredible tool for finding your purpose in life because they give you a complete picture of everything that's ever happened to you.

The Akashic Records were created before the universe was formed, and they contain every thought, word, and deed throughout eternity. Your records will tell you how all of your thoughts come into being and how they affect your life. The Akashic Records will also show you what purpose your thoughts have and why the universe gives you certain experiences in life.

So, if you feel lost or confused about what your next step should be, it might help to consult the Akashic Records for guidance.

IMPORTANCE OF FINDING YOUR PURPOSE

People spend their whole lives looking for a meaning to their life that often seems nonexistent. They try to force meaning on their life by needing to do something great or important to feel that they have a purpose. But the truth is, you already have a purpose for being here. It's not up to you to decide your purpose; that was decided before you even came into being.

Many people don't find a purpose for their life because they ask the wrong questions. They start by asking, "What do I want to accomplish in my lifetime?" or "How can I make this world better?" However, it's problematic to create your life mission based on what we think society sees as important.

It would be like repeating the same day over and over again for eternity. This would drive anyone crazy because they could never come up with what they wanted to do forever, and they'd eventually lose all meaning in life.

The truth is, there are no right or wrong questions when it comes to getting a glimpse of your life purpose. It's not about what you can do to help other people or make the world a better place. All these things are important, but they're not your true purpose because your life is already tied to all of them through cause and effect.

People ask the wrong questions for a few reasons: They're afraid to look at their true purpose in life because it'll make them feel more vulnerable; they want to live up to other people's expectations about what their purpose should be; or they're ashamed of themselves and think they need to change for their life to have a purpose.

When you ask the wrong questions, it will make you search for an answer that isn't there. You'll feel as if your life has no meaning and that nothing will ever work out the way you want it to. This can lead to depression and anxiety because you feel like your life is stuck in the same place. You won't be able to see that you already have everything you've been looking for, but all of it is waiting for you to find a better way of asking questions about yourself.

It's important to understand your true purpose in life because it will shape your entire life journey. If you don't know your purpose in life, then it's easy to lose sight of what you need to do.

Realizing your purpose in life will help you find the motivation and strength you need to take action in the world. It can also motivate others around you - which is an essential part of having a powerful influence on people. If you don't know the meaning behind your thoughts and life experiences, then it's easy to get lost in a whirlwind of confusion.

Yet, the Akashic Records are an invaluable resource when it comes to finding our purpose in life. The Records can show us how our thoughts come into being and how they affect our lives. They also show us what purpose these thoughts have and why the universe gives us various experiences in life.

The Akashic Records will show you how your destiny has unfolded throughout time. And it can help you understand why certain things happen in your life- like failures or success.

THE PERSONAL RECORDS

The Personal Records from the Akashic Records can be very useful for finding out why certain things happen in our lives. The reason for this is because they show us how our destiny unfolded throughout time. The Records can show us the cause and effect of what we do. For instance, if we're looking at a situation that didn't turn out the way we wanted it to, then there's a good chance it has something to do with our self-esteem or fears from our past coming up in the situation.

The Personal Records also give us knowledge about what kind of person we are and why certain characteristics and traits exist within ourselves. For example, if you want to find out why you feel unhappy all the time, then it's easy to ask a question like, "What happened in my past lives that made me want to feel unhappy all the time?" The Records will show us what kind of person we are when dealing with our emotions and how our thoughts affect our mood.

The Personal Records can give us a complete picture of our life. They can show us why we're afraid of certain things in our lives, and what we need to do to go after the person or situation we're fearing. It's easy to think, "I'm not good enough," but there's a reason for that belief existing within us. Chances are, it has something to do with an experience we had in life - like being ignored, rejected, or bullied by someone. The Akashic Records contain this information to find the answer to why we feel the way we do.

The Akashic Records are a place of absolute truth and honesty about who you are as a person and how your thoughts affect your destiny. It's easy to believe that the things that happen in our lives are random and have nothing to do with us. However, this isn't true because everything is created with a purpose and meaning through the Akashic Records.

The purpose of the Records is to help you understand yourself better to improve your life and relationships with others. You're meant to use the Records as a mirror and reflect on your thoughts to see why they exist within you.

The Akashic Records tell us that we don't need to push ourselves into thinking positively all the time because negativity isn't a bad thing. When it comes to reflecting on our lives in the Records, it's not only about finding out what's right about ourselves but also what's wrong. The purpose behind negativity is to humble us and teach us to be better people. Negative thoughts are like a mirror that reflects who you are on the inside - which can be incredibly hard to see at times.

THE SPIRITUAL PURPOSE

The spiritual purpose is, for the most part, something we all have in common. It's what connects us on a spiritual level to one another and can offer us tremendous insight when it comes to finding our true purpose in life. The Akashic Records are a place of absolute truth and honesty about who you are as a person and how your thoughts affect your destiny. It's easy to believe that the things that happen in our lives are random and have nothing to do with us. However, this isn't true because everything is created with a purpose and meaning through the Akashic Records.

One of the main purposes behind spirituality is to live authentically and without fear, including accepting ourselves as we are, flaws included. The Records tell us that our purpose on

Earth is to learn and experience, which includes overcoming challenges. Another interesting purpose behind living authentically is dealing with negative thoughts and feelings from past lives. The Akashic Records help us understand why we have certain fears and beliefs in this life that we may not even know about.

The Records tell us that we're all meant to be spiritual creatures who have the ability to channel higher knowledge and guidance from our Higher Selves. The Records are an incredibly powerful tool for opening our minds and understanding ourselves better as humans because they allow us to reflect on past lives that affect who we are today.

THE PERSONAL PURPOSE

There are many ways to find your purpose in life. One of the most popular is through Akashic Records, a record of every event that has ever happened on Earth and in Heaven. The Akashic Records contain all the knowledge you could possibly imagine because they're not restricted by time or space like we are here on Earth.

People can ask questions about their lives and receive answers from their Higher Self through opening their Akashic Records. The Akashic Records are an incredible tool for finding your purpose in life because they give you a complete picture of everything that's ever happened to you so far.

It's up to you to decide how much information you want to see and what's relevant. Your Higher Self will not show you anything that isn't important or meaningful in some way. Once you open your Akashic Records, it's common for people to see their past lives and their present one. It's a little different for everyone, but most people start out looking into the past. It's like looking through a filtered lens that shows you everything in your life from a particular perspective. The perspective of this lens is that of your Higher Self, and it always points to what will help you grow spiritually and advance your soul evolution. People see their past lives to learn how they've been creating the circumstances of their present life. They can also discover what events occurred due to choices and actions from past and present lives.

As we live our lives, we experience many different situations where love is involved, such as going on dates or having romantic relationships. These are good examples of how we experience people who may have been in our lives before. These connections often don't make sense until we connect the dots and discover that someone is a past lover or soulmate. It can be an incredible feeling when you realize that the person you're spending time with now was your spouse in another life.

We can also discover who the people are that we're meant to learn from in this lifetime. If a person comes into our lives for whatever reason, there's probably an important lesson to be learned by being with them. There might not always be a direct relationship between someone you feel close to and your past lives, but there's most likely some meaningful lesson that was waiting to be learned.

It can also help see how events in your life happened because of past actions and choices. Stuff happens, and we make bad decisions sometimes, which results in unfortunate circumstances that are hard to deal with at the time. When something bad occurs, it's not always your fault. Even though we tend to blame ourselves when bad stuff happens, finding out the real reason why something happened helps us take responsibility for our actions and move forward.

Seeing past and present lives through the lens of the Akashic Records is useful because it helps people find the lessons they're meant to learn in this lifetime. When people can find the bigger picture of their lives and past experiences, it's easier for them to accept what happened and understand why it happened.

***

The Akashic Records give you a new perspective that makes sense out of all the chaos in your life so that you can move forward in a positive direction.

The purpose of your personal records is to show you what the Akashic Records of you as a person are. The Records are a place of absolute truth and honesty about who you are as a person and how your thoughts affect your destiny. It's easy to believe that the things that happen in our lives are random and have nothing to do with us. However, this isn't true because everything is created with a purpose and meaning through the Akashic Records.

The Records tell us that we're all meant to be spiritual creatures who have the ability to channel higher knowledge and guidance from our Higher Selves. The Records are an incredibly powerful tool for opening our minds and understanding ourselves better as humans because they allow us to reflect on past lives that affect who we are today.

The Personal Records can give us a complete picture of our life. They can show us why we're afraid of certain things in our lives and what we need to do to go after the person or situation we're fearing. It's possible that the reason you're afraid of something is because you were hurt by it or someone else in a past life.

People often take their experiences with other people personally and get stuck living in the past without truly understanding why they are that way. The Akashic Records will give you an honest look at yourself so you can forgive yourself for past mistakes.

The Records will show you how other people in your life are creating the experience of fear, anger, and self-pity that you're feeling right now. You can use this knowledge to help yourself feel better about who you are as a person and not be so hard on yourself for past mistakes or things that happened to you in the past. You can move forward in your life without being stuck in the past or fearful about how people might treat you. The Records will bring to the surface all hidden feelings and issues from previous lives that have affected who we are.

.

CHAPTER 7. AKASHIC RECORDS AND SPIRITUAL HEALING: USING YOUR PAST LIVES TO HEAL IN THE PRESENT

The Akashic Records hold the blueprint for each individual's evolution to their highest potential through numerous lifetimes where they learn from both successes and failures along the way. Everything about you is recorded there, including your karma or lessons to be learned - the very reason you are here today! The healing process begins by connecting with these energies so that we can release patterns no longer needed for our growth and reclaim the gifts that may have been suppressed or forgotten.

The Akashic Records can be accessed using various techniques, including meditation, ritual, and visualization. You will learn how to connect with these records and explore the many ways they can heal us physically, emotionally, mentally as well as spiritually.

SPIRITUAL HEALING

Spiritual healing is one of the most powerful ways to affect change in your life. It is a powerful and transformative experience that can heal your mind, body, and spirit. If you are in need of any healing, spiritual healing could be the answer you've been looking for.

You don't have to be spiritual or religious to benefit from this energy-healing technique. There are very specific techniques you can use to connect with the Akashic Records. Once these steps have been taken, it's easy to access and explore how energy-healing can heal you mentally, emotionally, and physically.

Spiritual healing can help with many things, including improving your relationships, getting rid of phobias, healing your body, and even alleviating diseases like cancer. With the assistance of the Akashic Records, you can heal your body at a spiritual level. You will examine why you need healing and how to change the energy within yourself that's holding those patterns in place.

Spiritual healing isn't something that happens overnight. It takes time and commitment and requires dedication on your part!

Many people are hesitant about spiritual healing because they feel it's only for "good" people. This couldn't be further from the truth! Everyone deserves to live a life free of pain and filled with happiness. Negative thoughts, feelings, and emotions can keep you stuck in old habits that aren't serving you anymore, but these patterns can be changed.

Spiritual healing can help you connect with your spirituality and open up to a higher power, regardless of what that may be. It's an experience anyone can benefit from.

Spiritual Healing And The Akashic Records

There are many different ways to access your past lives, including meditation and ritual. You will also learn about the importance of forgiveness when it comes to spiritual growth, as well as how it can help you heal in this lifetime.

Spiritual healing and the Akashic Records are two very powerful healing modalities that can work together or be used separately depending on your needs. When working with the Akashic Records, you can release patterns of limitation and regain gifts that may have been suppressed or forgotten.

The Akashic Records hold the blueprint for your spiritual and physical healing and how to heal those around you. Learning about past lives will enable you to explore why certain illnesses have manifested in this lifetime. You'll also learn how to change energy patterns, gain balance within yourself, and make long-lasting changes.

If you're ready to transform your life in the most powerful way possible, spiritual healing and the Akashic Records can be there for you every step of the way!

Different Ways of Spiritual Healing through the Akashic Records

With a little time and commitment, anyone can heal themselves with help from their past lives recorded on the Akashic Records.

One of the many ways of spiritual healing through the Akashic Records is connecting to it for self-exploration. It provides a way for you to examine why illnesses have manifested in this lifetime and how to change energy patterns within yourself that are holding these patterns in place.

The other way to heal oneself with help from the Akashic Records is by utilizing it for spiritual growth. When you discover your past lives and release patterns of limitation, this can help you achieve your highest potential. Not only does it provide insight into your past lives but also how they manifest in this life and why illnesses have shown up as well.

USING YOUR PAST LIVES TO HEAL IN THIS LIFETIME

We're here today because we have lessons to learn which will help us improve in this lifetime. Our past lives help us learn the lessons needed to grow spiritually and mentally as well as emotionally. The Akashic Records will show you what patterns keep you stuck in old habits that aren't serving you.

When working with the Akashic Records, you can release these negative energy patterns by forgiving yourself and others. Forgiveness will allow you to let go of the hurt, anger, and resentment associated with these patterns so that you can move forward without the weight holding you back.

As an additional benefit, forgiving those who have hurt or offended you helps your energy flow more freely. This gives you a better chance at attracting love into your life, friendships, and even your career. Forgiveness also helps you release old habits and move forward with the positive, life-affirming changes needed to grow stronger personally and spiritually.

It's easy to become overwhelmed when faced with so many different things that masquerade as spiritual healing but connecting with the Akashic Records is the real deal. It's a healing process that anyone can learn to use and enjoy for many years to come. In fact, it will change your life in ways that you may have never imagined!

USING THE AKASHIC RECORDS FOR SELF-EXPLORATION

There are many ways to begin exploring your energy patterns, such as dream analysis, meditation, and visualization. When you connect with the Akashic Records to assist in this exploration, you'll find answers that have previously eluded you. You can also work with the Records using psychics, mediums, and counselors, to name a few.

As a way of beginning your exploration, consider connecting with your past lives through meditation or visualization to explore why certain things occurred in those lifetimes so that they are no longer affecting you today.

During this meditation or visualization, you may discover that you were involved with negative energy patterns such as abuse of alcohol and drugs, illness, depression, or physical ailments. This helps you to understand what caused the illnesses in this lifetime so that they can be resolved more easily.

To heal these energy patterns, it's helpful to connect with the Records to help you recognize the lessons learned in past lives. Then, forgive yourself and others so that these patterns can be released and your energy is flowing freely once again! This will allow you to move forward with more positive life-affirming changes and achieve your highest potential.

As time goes on, you'll gain an understanding of what's happening within your energy field and why certain illnesses, relationships, or careers have shown up. You'll also understand your patterns better so that you can move forward with the positive changes needed to grow stronger personally as well as spiritually!

USING THE AKASHIC RECORDS FOR SPIRITUAL GUIDANCE

It's a myth that only highly intelligent people are creative. In fact, research shows that once you get beyond an IQ of about 120, which is just a little above average Even though intelligent people might have a little advantage, intelligence is not required for creativity. That means that even if you're no smarter than most people, you still have the potential to wield amazing creative powers.

So why are so few people highly creative? Because there are bad habits people learn as they grow up, which crush the creative pathways in the brain. And like all bad habits, they can be broken if you are willing to work at them.

The Akashic Records are a great help here because they show you why those bad habits were put there in the first place so that you can clear them out of your brain and let your creativity flow freely.

Now, I'm not just talking about mindless daydreaming or doodling on a napkin. I'm talking about genuinely creative work that will stand the test of time.

Here's how it works. First, you need to learn to go into a deep meditative state, which is something everyone can do once they've learned how. After all, we were doing it easily as kids before our parents told us to stop wasting our time with such nonsense.

While you're in that deep meditative state, imagine yourself floating above the world and looking down on it. This is how we see the Akashic Records: as an enormous library containing every book written, movie made, song sung, and piece of music ever played. It's also how we find any specific book or episode within a movie or song.

Once you've found the book, movie, or song you're looking for, go inside and read page one. You'll discover why certain creative desires were programmed into your brain in that lifetime so that you could experience them for yourself to move forward along the spiritual path.

By forgiving yourself for any unconscious mistakes made and then resolving to avoid repeating them in the current lifetime, your creative pathways are freed up to do what they were put there for: create beautiful works of art that enrich lives and build bridges between people.

If you want to be unapologetically creative, then ask yourself this question: "Why am I here?" And make sure it's not just to make money or be famous. Those are common goals, but they don't lead you down the spiritual path that leads to self-realization and deep satisfaction in life.

The purpose of life is not to be happy as such but rather to love whatever you do. And I firmly believe that if we all channel our creativity into writing and painting and making music for others, the world would become a far better place.

If you've been feeling confused about your role on the planet, or if you're tired of feeling like a hamster on a wheel chasing material goals that never seem to be enough, the Akashic Records can help. They are your connection with higher levels of consciousness where you can receive inner guidance on what needs to change in your life so that you stop repeating the same mistakes and start making real progress on the spiritual path.

***

The Akashic Records are a set of teachings that hold the blueprint for what each individual can accomplish and evolve into. These records include our entire life, including karma or lessons to be learned - the very reason why we're here today! The healing process begins by connecting with these energies so that unwanted patterns, as well as gifts, maybe released to reclaim any potential lost through suppression or forgetfulness.

The Akashic Records are not buried deep in a library, as they are so vast that it would take lifetimes to find what you were looking for. Some people advise using meditation to tap into these energies and then searching through your mind's eye; however, this may or may not be the most effective way. Others suggest that the easiest way to find what you are looking for is by asking, "What is the lesson I have come here to learn?"

You may be a very spiritual and open-minded person who is happy to accept the teachings of past lives into your life, but what about your family, friends or co-workers? These questions may arise in the mind of an individual before they begin their journey: "Does everyone have them?", "What impact will this have on people around me?", "How many past lives have I had?" and "Are my experiences real or just my imagination?".

Using one's own life experiences plus their feelings surrounding them in a particular lifetime will help ensure that you discover your lesson quickly and effectively, as every event has a consistent feeling surrounding it within our Akashic Records.

Chapter 8. Opening Doors and Passing between Worlds: Connect with Your Akashic Records

An Akashic reader enters into what's known as the Akashic Realm, where they can access these memories and read them like books on shelves with titles such as past life readings, karma readings, soul contract readings, etc. This is not a place for someone without training to venture into because it can be very dangerous. They must know how to protect themselves from all the energies that are there. It is literally like walking into a spiritual library with books stacked on shelves and tables with no librarian around. People will often hear things in their mind as if someone is whispering, but they aren't sure where it's coming from, what it's about, or if they should listen to it. It can also be that they feel pulled in a certain direction and don't know what's calling them but have this strong desire to go there. This is the akashic realm trying to draw them into its space where all these energy signatures are located and directed at everyone who enters. A trained reader knows how to avoid them and shield themselves from them to perform their reading. If they have not developed these skills, they will get sick and be less effective at their readings because of the interference of the energies in that realm. Remember that time does not exist there as it does here in physical reality, so one can literally go back into their own past lives to the exact date and time they are interested in reading about.

PART 1 FOCUSING YOUR SEARCH

Create your agreements to help you remain committed to your process of accessing the Akashic Records. If you do not create a structure in how you intend to receive information, it is difficult for anyone to do an Akashic Records reading to understand your intention. This can lead to unnecessary confusion and frustration. Try taking a few minutes before entering the meditative state to write down what you want from the session. Don't be afraid of being too detailed or specific with questions, as this is one way to help identify specific blocks, lessons, and fears regarding the past life. If you are using a pen or pencil, make sure to use permanent ink.

IDENTIFY YOUR INTENTIONS FOR ACCESSING THE AKASHIC RECORDS.

Think about why you want to open your Akashic records and the type of knowledge you are seeking. You can also ask your guides to help you narrow down what knowledge is relevant. How much information do you want? What will you do with the information once you receive it? What are your expectations for this experience? Are there any blocks or fears that may come up and affect the outcome of your session? These questions are great because they help create intention, which is vital for accessing the Akashic Records. Write down your intentions.

WRITE DOWN ANY SPECIFIC QUESTIONS ABOUT YOUR PAST LIFE.

If you intend to access information regarding a specific past life, writing down questions about that particular life will help you narrow what you need. Keep in mind that the Akashic Records contain all information related to your spiritual journey and not just one area.

ASK QUESTIONS THAT CAN HELP YOU DECIDE YOUR CURRENT LIFE.

Ask questions about the current life's lessons, blockages, and healing. What is your soul's purpose? What fears are holding you back from achieving this goal? What can you do to eliminate these blocks so that you may receive more abundance in your life? Write down an affirmation related to past or current life knowledge that resonates with you. Affirmations are positive statements that aid in manifesting the knowledge you requested.

TRY ASKING ONE QUESTION AT A TIME TO FOCUS MORE.

If you have too many questions to ask in one session, try splitting them into smaller sections and asking each question one by one. If you intend to receive information about a past life, you can create a list of questions related to specific things or events that occurred during this life. You can use these questions to guide you through the process of the session. If you have several questions, it helps greatly to number them to be easily identifiable and recorded during your session.

PART 2 ENTERING A RECEPTIVE STATE

Visualization is used to prepare the mind and body for a meditative state that can be used to access the Akashic Records. This section will help you understand the importance of visualizing your guide or spirit companions so that they may aid you in traveling to the Akashic Realm. Visualization also helps you dive deeper into the meditative state and could be used for grounding after the session.

You can say your blessing for your guides to help you with the session and ask them for their permission to proceed. By allowing your guides to help you access the Akashic Records, you will receive the most relevant information and guidance for current life issues.

CLEAR OUT ANY NEGATIVE ENERGY IN YOUR SYSTEM BEFORE THE SESSION BEGINS.

We recommend clearing out any clutter or distracting areas in your home or room where you will be meditating. To clear out negative energy, you can burn some sage or use a spray bottle filled with water and a few drops of rosemary essential oil to surround yourself with an energy clearing shield before entering your Akashic Records session.

STATE YOUR INTENTION OR QUESTION ALOUD AND ASK FOR GUIDANCE.

Before entering the Akashic Records, it is helpful to establish a set intention. By stating your intention out loud, you allow yourself to enter a more receptive state to receiving information for what you are seeking. State your soul's highest and best potentials by asking about lessons experienced in a past life or current life's fears that you are ready to let go of and move beyond. This is a wonderful way to clear the subconscious mind of doubts or fears that may be holding you back from moving forward in your life path.

SIT OR LIE DOWN IN A COMFORTABLE, QUIET PLACE.

Sit or lie down in a comfortable, quiet place where you will not be disturbed. You may want to sit in a cross-legged position or on your bed with pillows and blankets under you for support and comfort. Make sure that you have no distractions during the session to focus solely on accessing information from your Akashic Records.

ASSUME A COMFORTABLE POSITION FOR YOU TO MEDITATE.

Close your eyes and take several deep breaths or even do some light physical exercise, such as walking around the block to enter an alpha brain wave state and release any stress in your system before attempting to access information from the Akashic Records.

CREATE A SACRED SPACE FOR YOURSELF.

By creating space and sacredness, you allow room and honor the moment of receiving this information from the Akashic Records. This will help you enter your more receptive state during the session because it shows that you respect what is happening.

OPEN THE DOOR WITH THE PRAYER OF THE PATHWAY.

You can use this prayer to help open the door between worlds. This is a great way to begin your journey by aligning your energy with these higher realms and preparing yourself for receiving information from the Akashic Records. You can make your own, or you may use the following Pathway Prayer by Linda Howe:

Opening Prayer
1. And so, we do acknowledge the Forces of Light
2. Asking for guidance, direction, and courage to know the Truth
3. As it is revealed for our highest good and the highest good of
4. Everyone connected to us.
5. Oh, Holy Spirit of God,
6. Protect me from all forms of self-centeredness
7. And direct my attention to the work at hand.
8. Help me to know (myself) in the Light of the Akashic Records,
9. To see (myself) through the eyes of the Lords of the Records,

10. And enable me to share the wisdom and compassion that the Masters, Teachers, and Loved Ones of (me) have for (me).

11. The Records are now open.

Say lines 1–10 of the Opening Prayer aloud. Repeat lines 8–10 silently two more times using your current legal name. Announce the opening of the Records by saying line 11 aloud.

MEDITATE ON YOUR QUESTION WHILE IN YOUR DEEPLY RELAXED STATE.

Meditate on your question until you feel a blockage or resistance. The first thing that comes to mind is usually the first answer that pops into your mind. Go with this inner knowing, even if it doesn't seem logical in some way. This is because you are accessing information from the Akashic Records, which provides answers based not on your current reality but on how they best serve you. The Akashic Records are like the fabric of life and therefore have all possible answers to any question that you may ask.

ASK TO BE GRANTED ACCESS TO THE AKASHIC RECORDS.

Once you have meditated for five minutes or longer, ask for permission to enter the Akashic Records. You may do this by saying: "I request permission to be granted access to information that is held in the fabric of life, which is called the Akashic Records. I have a question that I wish to gain information on and would like assistance with my search." Then, just relax.

When you feel relaxed, you will be able to access information from Akashic Records. In your session, you may feel several things, including:

- Peaceful energy around you
- A presence of energy near or in front of you
- A sensation of rising to another realm
- Emotional shifts within you
- Disorientation
- Visions of past lives, perhaps with a strong feeling of being in that life or body and reliving feelings, senses, scent, sounds, sights
- A re-emergence into the physical form after an out-of-body experience
- A sense of calming when you arrive in this realm of the Akashic Records
- A sense of being surrounded by others, perhaps family or guides who assist with your session

WAIT FOR INFORMATION TO COME INTO YOUR CONSCIOUSNESS.

When you feel relaxed and ready, ask your question aloud or think your question silently in your mind. Give yourself about 10 seconds to receive an answer that comes to mind. Don't allow any doubts or fears to stop you from getting an answer.

Introduce yourself and repeat your question to anyone you encounter.
When you receive that answer, ask your question again and wait for the next information to come to mind. Sometimes, this will be an image or a few words. Write it down as soon as possible. Ask for a sentence about what you just received or ask for more detail on what you just recorded.

Ask for another sentence or two and record it. Continue this process with each answer that comes into your consciousness until you feel the session is complete. You may find that you receive answers in a series of short sentences instead of one large paragraph, which can be just as valuable if not more so. Sometimes, the answers are not intellectual. Record what you got, then see if you can make sense of it after your session is complete. You may even find that no matter how hard you try to understand something or put words to your experience that there is nothing more that comes to mind or that things still don't seem clear to you. This is fine and natural, and you may just have to wait for more information or integrate the experience in other ways, such as using your intuition with this new piece of information that came into your life.

Leave the Akashic Realm with a closing prayer.
When you feel a natural shift, such as your consciousness returning to the physical realm, or you feel that it's time to end this experience, say goodbye to any guides and helpers who are with you. Thank them for their assistance and guidance. Consider closing the session with gratitude. Read the Closing Prayer aloud.

Closing Prayer

I would like to thank the Masters, Teachers, and Loved Ones for their love and compassion.
I would like to thank the Lords of the Akashic Records for their point of view.
And I would like to thank the Holy Spirit of Light for all knowledge and healing.
The Records are now closed. Amen.
The Records are now closed. Amen.
The Records are now closed. Amen.

PART 3 INTERPRETING WHAT YOU FIND

After the experience, you should now process your experience and integrate your new information. You may want to journal or write down what you experienced, felt, and heard. For some, recording the experience is easy enough to record everything as it comes in during the session. Others need to take more time after their sessions are complete before organizing their thoughts and integrating what they learned from the Akashic Records. Record whatever came into your consciousness.

OPEN YOUR EYES AND REORIENT YOURSELF TO YOUR SURROUNDINGS.

When your session is complete, come back into the physical realm. Open your eyes and take a deep breath. Thank whoever you encountered during this process for the assistance they provided to you on your quest. Give yourself time to adjust before making any decisions about what you learned from accessing information in the Akashic Records. Your answers will always be most useful when they are applied to your current life and not as a mystical concept.

REFLECT ON THE EXPERIENCE AFTER YOU FINISH YOUR MEDITATION.

When you are ready, record what you learned about your question. Go back over it a few times until the information becomes clear in your mind once more. Then, apply this knowledge into your life for at least three months before deciding if you felt better (or worse) as a result.

Write down what you learned during your experience with the Akashic Records in case it is helpful to you at a later date. Know that this information will help you, even if it doesn't feel like it at first glance. It may take a few days or weeks before you feel its effects in your life.

REPEAT THE PROCESS REGULARLY TO CONTINUE LEARNING MORE.

If you are uncomfortable with the information, ask for a new session to be conducted again and the Akashic Records to be updated on your request. If you are happy with the results, repeat your question to keep learning more.

Occasionally, you will find that an answer is not complete, and a follow-up session must be made. This is common while accessing information in the Akashic Records.

BE HONEST WITH WHAT YOU THINK AND FEEL.

The Akashic Records will give you an answer to your question, but it may not be what your mind expects or what the ego wants to hear. If this is the case, do not accept the information as truth until you process it in a way that feels natural for you.

Remember that when it comes to the Akashic Records, there are no wrong answers. What you received is likely to apply in your life or will be useful at a later time, so trust what you discover from this process and keep it with you for future reference.

If you disagree with the information you received while accessing the Akashic Records, do nothing about it until at least three months have passed. If your answer still feels wrong, you may need to ask for a new session or rephrase your question.

It is possible that you will receive information with which you cannot live in harmony. This can cause feelings of confusion or even anger. If this happens, write down the emotions you are feeling and then release them. Remain open-minded about all that you receive from the Akashic Records, even if it does not fit your current beliefs.

Asking for assistance before and during the Akashic Records session is highly recommended. You may find that the presence of others in a group setting can help keep you more focused and relaxed while accessing these records. If this feels right for you, ask a friend to meditate with you or call on someone you feel will provide positive energy while you connect with the Akashic Records.

Feel free to share your experience with others who may be interested.

All experiences are equally valid and valuable. All that matters is that you feel a sense of peace.

***

If you've never tapped into the power of your Akashic Records before, it can seem overwhelming to know how. It may take a few tries or more than one session until you have success connecting with your Akashic Records in your meditation sessions, but if this is something that interests you, then we encourage staying at it! The best way to learn about the world around us is by doing our research and trying things out. So be open-minded when reading up on these types of topics and don't hesitate to try new things!

.

Chapter 9. Opening the Akashic Records for Others: Enlightenment at Your Fingertips

Previous chapters in this book have talked about how you can open your Akashic Record and call forth your own past lives experiences to help achieve enlightenment. But what if someone else wants to see their life lessons, and what if they don't want to do the work of opening a past life themselves? Is there a way that you, as someone who believes in reincarnation, can help them get answers without forcing them to look for themselves or without getting yourself involved in anything that could possibly be harmful to them? The answer is yes. And it's a simple yes, not to be confused with an overly complicated one that requires hard work and sacrifice from you.

Opening the Akashic Records for others is a service that can help people make better decisions in their lives. It's also an enlightening experience that helps you open up to your power as a creator. We explore what opening the Akashic Records entails and how it can be beneficial to those who are willing to try it. We'll also discuss some of the common assumptions about opening the Akashic Records for others. Hence, you know what you're getting into before deciding if this is something worth exploring further. For clarity from hereon, the term "requester" will be used to refer to the person asking you to open their Akashic records on their behalf.

ADDITIONAL THINGS TO CONSIDER WHEN OPENING THE AKASHIC RECORDS FOR OTHERS:

OBTAINING CONSENT IS NECESSARY AND FOREMOST.

You may feel called to do this service for a particular person, but before doing any readings, make sure that you have consent from the requester. It's your moral and ethical duty to ask the requester if they are willing to receive an Akashic Record reading and how they wish their information shared with you.

Most of your requesters will probably be happy to give you consent as a way of honoring the healing that they hoped to receive from you. By opening Akashic Records for others, the requesters are not only trusting your ethics and moral values but also enabling you to expand your insight as a healer, thus helping them benefit from an even more powerful service.

It's also important to note that paying attention to your ethics and moral values is important when you're opening the Akashic Records for others, as you may feel called to share your knowledge with other healers or counselors. Be sure that whatever decision you make in this regard is well-thought-out before making any commitments.

CONFIDENTIALITY IS OF UTMOST IMPORTANCE.

Some of your requesters may be willing to let you share their information with other trusted healers or counselors, and that's perfectly fine. However, if they don't want their information to be shared with anyone else, prefer not to have any written notes made about them and don't wish for the reading session recorded in any way (including audio recordings), be sure to respect their wishes. Follow up about it after the reading is done, and let them know if you could honor their wishes in that regard.

PRESENT THE INFORMATION YOU RECEIVED CONCISELY.

You may feel that some of the information you see has a direct cause-and-effect relationship, but be aware that it's best to present your requester with non-judgmental language when discussing what you saw in their Akashic Records. It would be wise to use words like "it looks like" or "you experienced" rather than "this is the reason why."

You should also avoid statements like "you have" or "you are" because it has a negative connotation as if you were labeling your requester. Instead, try saying, "it looks like you experienced (or had) X in your past life or incarnation." Another thing to consider is that some of your requesters may react negatively if you bring up something in their past. Avoid this as much as possible by simply saying what you saw without attaching a label to it or putting it into words for the requester.

PREPARE FOR ANY EMOTIONS THAT COME OUT DURING THE READING.

It's normal to feel uncomfortable when bringing up certain issues and topics. If you're feeling uncomfortable with what the Akashic Records are showing you about your requester, be sure to let them know so they can understand where it's coming from. Also, if any strong emotions come out during the session, stay in a non-judgmental space and recognize that these feelings are coming from both yourself and the requester.

MINORS ARE EASILY SWAYED.

If your requester is a minor or someone who is barely an adult, be aware that they may not have enough of a sense of self to understand what truly happened in their past lives. If possible, let your requester know about how they experienced certain things so they can form their own opinion on it, but leave it at that. As earlier mentioned, only those above 18 years of age are allowed to access their Records.

STEPS IN OPENING THE AKASHIC RECORDS FOR OTHERS

Remember how you opened your Akashic Records? The process is still the same. The main difference is that you're opening the Records for another person instead of yourself. Be sure that you intend to help them and not for any selfish reasons. If you're doing this for the wrong reason, it will come back to haunt you, so make sure you know why you're doing it before proceeding.

Take note of the changes you need to make personally when opening the Records for others. You must put the requester's needs first, focusing on how the Records will be beneficial to them. Walk them through the first part to zero in on the question and create the agreements. Ensure that the requester fully understands the process, and proper expectations are set. Once you get to the second part, encourage participation in visualizing and blessing. When you read the Prayer of the Pathway, say lines 1–10 of the Opening Prayer aloud, with the requester's preferred name. Repeat lines 8–10 silently two more times using the requester's current legal name. Announce the opening of the Records by saying line 11 aloud. The information you will receive does not belong to you, so avoid adding personal context to it. You may get confused by what you will see, but remember you are not in the position to make sense of the requester's Records. After closing the session, disorientation might set in, so it is advised to do a grounding activity to regain your bearings.

So here's an easy step by step guide on what you need to do to facilitate this:

#1. Ask your friend if they're open to opening their Akashic Record and receiving information from past lives.

#2. If they say yes, help them relax by guiding them into a state of meditation (or whatever form of relaxation that works for them like yoga or chanting). Make sure that they are fully in a relaxed state.

#3. After relaxation, continue by guiding the person to picture them standing in the middle of a room filled with light as you begin to call forth their Akashic Record into your own hands and transfer it into theirs as you say: "The Akashic Records are now open for (insert name) to see all their past lives as a way of finding the answers to guide them in this lifetime. May they use this information wisely."

#4. If you are not sure if your friend is ready for the experience of having their Akashic Record opened, then you can stop here and let them know that there's no rush and that they can come back to this when they are ready.

#5. If they are ready, then you can have them lay down on a flat surface or their bed as you open your own Akashic Record and allow the energies of what is in there to be transferred into yours. Let it flow naturally as it will. Make sure that you have them in a safe environment and under the supervision of someone who is fully trusted.

#6. Once you have done that, ask your friend to open their eyes and tell them what they saw. You can also encourage them to make notes of anything that might help with the interpretation later on if they are not ready for any immediate revelations at this time.

#7. Once they have their interpretation, help them to put it into context with what is already going on in their life or the parts that are unclear.

#8. Then leave them alone and allow them time to absorb everything and confirm if this is true for themselves, by themselves.

#9. They should then come back to you and let you know if they need any more help.

#10. But before leaving them, make sure to thank them for their time and effort as it will greatly help them get a better understanding of who they really are and why they are here in this lifetime. Then help them create a plan of how they can apply everything that was revealed to them today and have them commit to it by saying something like: "As of this day and time, I fully accept the fact that my Akashic Record is open to me. And from now on, I will do everything in my power to record everything that I've learned here today and apply them in my life."

Again, if your friend is not ready for this process, then make sure that they come back to it when they are in a state of readiness. Some people might just need some time to accept the idea of reincarnation first before attempting to do anything like this.

Many requesters will end up feeling relieved after having a session with you, but some may also feel discomfort and find their life changing in significant ways because of the information they received from the Akashic Records. Although some people are able to accept these changes right away, others might take time to integrate them before making any decisions. Allow them some time to absorb the information and then check with them to see if they need any more help.

The most important thing for you to remember is that all these changes are a normal process of self-discovery because people have different ways of dealing with their new worldview after being exposed to this type of information.

There are two primary ways in which opening the Akashic Records for others can reveal information: The first way is by having someone else go through their personal Akashic Record on their behalf to read everything that's in it. This type of reading is done by connecting with the Records and channeling the information into a physical, tangible form so it can be seen by someone else (the requester). The second way is for you to do this alone as you go inside your Records to gain insight on what was going on in a certain lifetime or why the requester is currently experiencing such thoughts and feelings. But it should be noted that using only one method can still provide you with enough information to answer questions for your requester.

COMMON ASSUMPTIONS

There are several assumptions that people make about opening the Akashic Records for others. Here are some of the most common ones:

OPENING THE AKASHIC RECORDS CAN ONLY BE DONE IF YOU'RE FORMALLY TRAINED IN THIS FIELD.

The truth is, anyone with a desire to do so can open up their own personal Records and gain access to past information that will help them get a better understanding of who they are and why they're here in this lifetime.

OPENING THE AKASHIC RECORDS ISN'T SAFE.

It's true that there are various risks to opening the Akashic Records for others (we don't recommend that you do it alone), but with proper training, precautions can be taken before a session begins to make sure no harm comes to you or the requester.

OPENING THE AKASHIC RECORDS MEANS THAT A PERSON'S LIFE WILL BE COMPLETELY CHANGED.

While it is true that people can gain some new insights from what they're shown during an opening the Akashic Records session, their lives don't have to change dramatically because of it. In fact, for most people, having their Records opened doesn't mean having a complete life makeover; it's more like an expansion of awareness that can help them gain a deeper understanding of themselves.

OPENING THE AKASHIC RECORDS MEANS YOU'LL NO LONGER HAVE TO SUFFER IN THIS LIFETIME.

Although we believe that opening the Akashic Records for others can provide people with a better understanding of why they're experiencing certain events, it doesn't mean that those things will completely disappear from their lives.

OPENING THE AKASHIC RECORDS MEANS BECOMING PSYCHIC.

While this info can help you feel more in-tune with your being, it doesn't make you psychic because no one really knows what the future holds or what will happen to them at any given point.

OPENING THE AKASHIC RECORDS MEANS SEEING EVERYTHING THAT HAS EVER HAPPENED OR IS HAPPENING NOW.

This is true for some people, but not for everyone else. Opening the Akashic Records can provide you with a lot of information about your past lives (which might seem like they are right here and now), but that doesn't mean you'll be able to see the present or future.

***

Your spiritual journey is a mysterious one. It can be hard to find your purpose in this world when there are so many distractions and obstacles in your life. Many people seek out answers but don't really know what they're looking for. Others aren't sure how to ask the right questions or interpret the information that comes to them. Opening the Akashic Records for others is a service that can help people make better decisions in their lives. It's also an enlightening experience that helps you open up to your power as a creator, but only if done with pure intentions and goodwill towards all parties involved.

The information contained in an individual's Akashic Records can be applied to other people, places, and events. When working with requesters on their Akashic Records, we often find that there are past-life connections and connections between people in this lifetime. This helps explain why certain things keep happening to us or why it seems like some people are always in our lives. Past-life connections are rarely random, as we can see when patterns of behavior repeat themselves between lifetimes.

.

CHAPTER 10. MEDITATION AND THE AKASHIC RECORDS: REWRITING YOUR LIFE STORY

It's a common misconception that meditation is all about emptying the mind. In fact, it's just as much about filling your head with positive thoughts and memories from which you can draw strength and inspiration. And one of the most powerful ways to do this is by tapping into the Akashic Records.

But how can it be possible for a human being to tap into something so vast and deep? The answer is by opening your mind to meditation. And there are numerous ways to do this, including the practice of living in the present moment, grounding yourself in your body with yoga or other bodywork such as massage, enhancing your creativity through art and music (by playing a musical instrument, for example), and focusing on what's truly important to you in life.

The key is simply to let go of all thoughts, emotions and sensations – both physical and conceptual. So, when you're doing daily meditation, try to focus purely on the present moment without thinking about anything else, including your past or future; the Akashic Records will automatically come into play once you cross this point of no return.

To help you do this, you could start every session with the following affirmation: I am ready to access the Akashic Records and draw upon their wisdom. From now on, my consciousness will be open to all of the human knowledge.

Then just relax into your meditation space for 10 minutes or so every day and allow yourself to drift back through time until you reach the part of your life where you want to start looking for answers. The Akashic Records can show you anything – from how to find fulfilling work and relationships to the road map for world peace, from revealing your true purpose in life to showing you how to heal yourself or others.

When you sense that it's time to move on, return your consciousness to the present moment. And then, go back to the beginning of your session and repeat this process until you feel ready to finish working with the Akashic Records. At this point, you can affirm that they will continue helping you whenever you need them and then finish up by saying thank you for all their help.

Once you get into this cycle of work and rest, you'll find that the Akashic Records have a way of speaking to you – and the more often you connect with them in this way, the clearer their words will become. So don't be surprised if your meditation experience feels very real indeed: it is real but on a different level of reality. And if you're working with the Akashic Records at this point in your life, there's no need to stop once you finish your daily session: all that will happen is that they'll keep bringing new insights and ideas into your consciousness whenever their assistance is required.

An Open Heart Meditation to Receive Spiritual Guidance in Preparation for Accessing Your Akashic Records

Open heart meditation is designed to help you open your heart to receive spiritual guidance and wisdom from spirit guides.

Find a comfortable place where you can either sit or lay down. Close your eyes and begin to relax, releasing the tension from the top of your head down to your toes.

Focusing on your breath, lengthening it, helping the breath heal the body, open the body, creating space, relaxation, openness. Now visualize, feel, or imagine a beautiful light at the top of your head. See this beautiful light entering from the crown of your head down into your head cavity into each and every part of your body. This light moves in a wave-like form, spreading into each and every cell of your body, releasing any tension, any contraction, any toxins, any thoughts, any trauma from each and every cell of your body, replacing it with light, with peace, with openness. As the light continues to move into each and every cell of your body, you feel more and more relaxed, more and more at peace, more and more.

Now bring your awareness to the space of your heart, right behind your heart center, at the very center of your chest. And as you maintain your awareness at the back of your heart, observe this space. Is it open and free of tension? Is it relaxed? How do you breathe into this space? Is it expanded? Intend to create more space.

More relaxation, more expansion in the space of your heart. You may smile to help that process. Smiling to your heart, and as you smile to each and every cell in your heart, your heart opens and expands. I imagine a vortex of energy flowing into your heart from the front of your heart clockwise and releasing through the back counterclockwise, moving the energy in the space of your heart, bringing in new energy, love, relaxation, healing, peace, and to the back releasing any trauma and fighting any toxins, any stress, any anxiety, any painful memory that has been recorded in your heart. As you visualize this beautiful swirl of energy moving in your heart, bringing in more and more love, more and more energy into the space of your heart, you see beautiful golden and green lights swirling together, taking you deeper and deeper into your heart center.

As you continue to move deeper and deeper into your heart center, you feel lighter, brighter, more expanded, more relaxed. You feel the space of your heart expanding so much that it's beyond the space of your physical body. Continue to smile to focus on the swirl of energy of beautiful golden and green lights moving deeper and deeper into your heart and feeling your heart expand more and more. As your heart continues to expand, open, and heal, maybe you become aware of some pain in your heart, something that has brought you pain, suffering, a past event that you're still holding on to. Once you've noticed that pain, maybe memories of it come to the surface, thoughts, images, physical sensations, notice them and allow them to release. Becoming aware that they were there, that they were stored. And choosing to let them go, to clear them, to release them from your heart, not as how when he let them go, your heart expands even more. There's more space; there's more relaxation; there's more room for new feelings, new emotions, new relationships. Continue to release any pain from your heart, allowing for your heart to expand more and more and continue to follow the swirl of beautiful golden and green lights right into the very center of your heart.

When you feel that you have reached the center of your heart, connect to the love that is there. Love coming from your soul. Feel how loved you are, how cared for you are, how supported you are, and note that you can always go back to the space in your heart and feel this level of love, of care, of support right at the center of your heart. Remaining in the center of your heart, think about something in your life that you'd like to improve, a situation that you'd like to change and make better.

And now, ask for guidance. Ask for your spirit guides, angels, masters, and ascended masters, anyone you feel connected to. Ask them for their help, their guidance. Is there anything they want to tell you, to share with you? Anything that will help you bring more love, joy, happiness, and inner peace in your life. Can they tell you; can they show you whether it's images, words, mind to mind connection or thoughts? Allow yourself to receive their message and connect to the vibration of this message. What it feels like inside of you when you receive this message? How do you feel as you connect deeply with the message that you're receiving by filling it to anchor, to integrate? For this vibration to be known by you, integrated into your consciousness and know that you can return to that state of deep peace, deep relaxation, that state of inner knowing any time you choose to, by going deep, deep into the space of your heart. Clearing and letting go of pain and opening your heart to being guided, being loved, and being supported. Now thank your guides, spirit guides, sending masters, angels, anyone who came forward to help you; guide you. Thank them for their help, and know that you can communicate with them anytime you come back to this space. Also, remember that the vibration that you felt when you got an answer to your question when you got a message is also always available to you by simply going into the space of your heart and tuning in, tuning into this vibration embodying it.

Now slowly coming back to the present moment, returning to the space you are in and the time you are in. Deepening your breath, feeling your heart expanded, and maintaining this expansion of your heart as you come back to the present moment. Begin to wiggle your fingers on your toes, and when you're ready, gently open your eyes.

Guided Meditation to Access the Akashic Records
This guided meditation for discovering your relationships, lives, and souls purpose will help you make a connection to the highest source of love and wisdom for your highest good. All you need to access the Akashic records is an open heart and an open mind rooted in love to ask your questions and rooted in acceptance to receive the answers. You must trust the universe to always work in your favor and support you every step of the way to assist and guide you into knowledge that will serve you in your soul's journey and in this meditation to discover your relationships, lives, and souls purpose.

So are you ready to tune in? Are you in a quiet place where you will be undisturbed and ideally after so you can reflect on this experience? Are you comfortable either sitting or lying down? Are you ready? Yes, good. As we prepare for our meditation, let's seek a moment to focus on the centering thought. Today and every day, I align my conscious, subconscious, and superconscious to live in alignment with my soul's purpose for my highest good and those of all. Today and every day, I align my conscious, subconscious, and superconscious to live in alignment with my soul's purpose for my highest good and those of all.

As we prepare to begin with deep breathing, imagine on each inhale, drawing in the energy that you have scattered out into the universe such as thoughts, concerns, or worries about the past or future, and on the exhale, imagine releasing any energy that you have taken on that does not belong to you, like other people's concerns or judgments, what they said, or what you think they may think, send it back to them. Returning to your center, allowing the tensions in your body to dissipate as you breathe slowly, so fill your lungs, think my energy back to me, and as you exhale, think others' energy back to them. Again, take a deep breath in, draw your energy back into you, and exhale with a long sigh, releasing the energy of others. One last time, inhale slowly and deeply, draw all of your energy back in, and exhale with a sigh, giving back all the energy that belongs to others. Good, now you can breathe normally. In a moment, I will be counting from 10 down to 1. With each descending number, you will become more attuned to shift vibrational energy to a state of heightened awareness. Closing your eyes now as I start the countdown.

Ten, listen to the sound. Nine, let the beat become your focus. Eight, listen with your whole being. Seven, let the rhythm fill your senses. Let it flow into you like waves. Six, let it resonate in every part of you riding the rhythm. Five, feel it in your blood and your bones. Four, feel the connection to the Earth rise, deep from under your feet, flowing up into your body, anchoring you as the beat becomes a part of you. Three, experience your separate identity dissolving physical limitations, disappearing, descending, and floating upwards at the same time. And one, experience yourself synchronizing with the heartbeat of the universe, with the rhythm of your being, sense this connection unfold as it unfolds. You may sense your verticality like a column of energy reaching down and up, pulsating, and vibrating like a pillar of light, maybe as wide as you're tall. Sense your energy, body stretching, imagine elongating up and down, expanding from the center and simultaneously in all directions, down, down, down, to the front, to the back, and to all sides as you extend your awareness further gradually. Time and space may disappear if you haven't already. You may sense limitations begin to dissolve. As boundaries are being lifted, you may perceive yourself as heavy yet weightless, fluid yet solid and strong, bringing you into a moving stillness. Here, you may become aware of a feeling of complete nothingness, yet nothing seems missing. It may seem as complete transparency, yet there's nothing to see. It may seem as nothing happens, yet everything is happening. As if you are in a place of infinity and beyond a place where heaven and earth meet within you. And as this connection amplifies a sense of peace, a calm knowingness spreads. Within you, that clarity, wisdom, and love are always available. From and within this place has the divine, loving, compassionate being that you are. From and within this place of higher wisdom and guidance, I will ask that loving, compassionate part of you questions to help you elicit your souls and tensions. Trust the answers, the vision, or the knowing that you receive. You do know the answers, and they will be revealed to you, if not now, within the next few days. It could be during a dream. It could be while you're walking outside, not even thinking about it. You could just get an epiphany and just to know. You will know, and the answers will come, remaining open and grateful.

Now think about a woman. Who is she? What can she teach you? What else can she teach you? What can you learn from her? What else can you learn from her? What about her brings you the most joy? What about her brings you the most pain? What does she really, deep down, want from you? What do you really deep down want from her? What is your purpose in her life? What is her purpose in your life? How does her life changed for the better as a result of having you in her life? How does your life change for the better as a result of having her in your life? What qualities does she bring out in you? What qualities do you bring out in her?

Now ask yourself, what are we here to create together? What are we here to heal in each other? What is the main theme of this relationship? Is it compassion, forgiveness, love, care, honesty, loyalty, freedom, power, or what is it? What are our sole purposes and being together? What are the necessary steps that I need to take to align to my soul's purpose now?

Good, now think about a man. Who is he? What can he teach you? What else can he teach you? What can you learn from him? What else can you learn from him? What about him brings you the most joy? What about him brings you the most pain? What does he really, deep down, want from you? What do you really, deep down, want from him? What is your purpose in his life? What is his purpose in your life? How does his life changed for the better as a result of having you in his life? How does your life change for the better as a result of having him in your life? What qualities does he bring out in you? What qualities do you bring out in him? Now ask yourself, what are we here to create together? What are we here to heal in each other? What is the main theme of this relationship: compassion, forgiveness, love, care, honesty, loyalty, freedom, power, or what is it? What are our sole purposes in being together? What are the necessary steps that I need to take to align to my soul's purpose now?

Now from within this higher place of wisdom and love, ask these soul questions. Who am I? Why am I here? What do I want? Good, now that you have your sole purpose as a state of being, can you see that your life purpose is contained within your soul purpose? Can you see now that your relationship purpose is already contained in the soul purpose? And finally, how does having a soul purpose transform your relationship with yourself and others as a way of being? You know the answers, and if they haven't already, they will be revealed to you. You will know, and the answers will come. Just keep reminding yourself of today's centering thought.

Today and every day, I align my conscious, subconscious, and superconscious to live in alignment with my soul's purpose for my highest good. Today and every day, I align my conscious, subconscious, and superconscious to live in alignment with my soul's purpose for my highest good. Today and every day, I align my conscious, subconscious, and superconscious to live in alignment with my soul's purpose for my highest good. The more you integrate this awareness, the more you evolve and remove the blocks to your path of highest self-realization and the true meaning of life. With this in mind, start bringing your awareness back into your body. Maybe stretch and move, wiggle a finger or toe, and when you feel ready, gently open your eyes and smile—feeling better? Maybe even better than in a long, long time about yourself, your life, and everyone in it.

You remember this entire session and you can return to it from anywhere any time you wish. It's often beneficial to keep a journal so you can reflect on what you experienced today.

MEDITATION GUIDE TO FINDING YOUR REAL LIFE PURPOSE

Make sure you'll be undisturbed. Dim the lights and lay or sit in a very comfortable position. Close your eyes and follow the sound of my voice. We're going on a visualized journey to see yourself performing activities, whatever they may be, fulfilling your purpose. Finding a purpose is not necessary during your lifetime. You may have incarnated here to have certain experiences and learn specific lessons. But if you feel you have a specific purpose but don't know what it is yet, it's likely that you do have one and intuitively know this is true.

First, I'll relax you down to allow your subconscious mind to step forward. Then we'll access your clairvoyance to bring wisdom in from your higher self. Here we go. I want you to allow yourself this time for yourself to concentrate on yourself. I want you to take a deep breath in now, and as you breathe out, allow any stresses and strains of daily life to leave you. Now gently breathe in again and as you breathe out, feel your facial muscles relaxed.

Breathe in again and as you breathe out, feel your shoulders drop and release all tension. And breathe in again, and as you breathe out, your arms grow heavy, and the tension just melts away. Breathe in again and as you breathe out, relax your chest and back muscles all the way down your back, and the last one now, focusing on the legs and the feet, breathe in and feel them totally relaxed.

As you breathe out, your body is very relaxed. Allow a warm feeling of calmness and tranquility to enter your mind. Allow this feeling to grow. You are very calm and peaceful, loved and protected, so you drift away, just drift away, drift deeper and deeper into a deep, deep feeling of relaxation. In a moment, I'll count you down and you will find yourself on a pathway in a beautiful green country scene.

Here we go, ten, nine, eight, seven, drifting deeper and deeper. Now six, five, four, three, drifting down, down. Two, one and find yourself there now on a pathway, in a beautiful country scene. The sun is shining and the air is a perfect temperature. Observe lush green trees around, grass, and little flowers. This really is a pleasant and comforting place. You feel very safe and protected here. Notice that the pathway stretches away, ahead of you. Begin walking down this lovely little path, observing the beauty all around you. Up ahead, you see something glowing, quite brightly in a magnificent golden, white light. As you continue walking, you see that up ahead, right on the path is a radiant doorway of light. The path leads straight up to this shining doorway with golden light streaming from it. This doorway is a portal to infinite knowing. Once you reach it, stand and face it and observe for a moment. On the other side of this portal, you'll be able to view yourself performing your purpose or perhaps more than one purpose, so just release any doubts or expectations. For a while, let the process unfold and just allow. So go ahead now and go through the doorway and know that this doorway will be right behind you as soon as you wish to return.

On the other side now, allow your surroundings to gently form for you. Accept what you see, whatever comes. If you could, observe yourself fulfilling your purpose now. What would you see? Observe yourself now and take a few moments to do so. Wonderful, just allow your surroundings to fade for you now, and I'm going to count you down from five to one. You will find yourself in new surroundings, observing yourself doing something else, some other purpose or activity that would be beneficial for you to perform in this lifetime.

Here we go, five, four, three, two, one, and find yourself there. Take a moment, allowing your surroundings to form. If you could see yourself performing other worthwhile actions, what do you see right now? Taking your time, allowing the scene to appear for you now, and take a few moments to observe you. Lovely, well done.

Now it's time to return. Turn around and see the glowing doorway of golden light behind you. Go ahead and walk through the doorway now and find yourself on the pathway in the beautiful country scene once more. Take a deep breath in now and breathe out. Head back along the pathway now, observing the beautiful surroundings as you walk along. As you go, thank your higher self for providing you with this insight into your purpose today and bring back with you only the insight you wish to keep. In a moment, I'll count you up, returning to normality.

Here we go, one, two, three, four, five, returning feeling calm and rested. Six, seven, eight, nine, ten, and return to normality feeling refreshed. You can open your eyes when ready.

GUIDED MEDITATION TO CLEARING KARMA

This guided meditation will give you the opportunity to let go, release, and break vows of poverty, celibacy, and suffering made in prior lives. Past life energy can follow us into this life. Whatever karmic energy is showing up right now, know that is not here to drag you down or to punish you. On the contrary, it can be used as a powerful stepping stone and healing opportunity for your highest good and devastating when you are fully committed to do the deep cleansing of multiple issues from multiple past lives. It also heals childhood and early adult with wounds from this life, including sexual traumas, addictions, relationship wounds, and business challenges.

Today, I will guide you in clearing, releasing, and breaking karmic agreements that block you from living in the highest excitement—releasing karma in all lifetimes, in all incarnations, past, present, and future on this planet in this reality and all other dimensions or levels of existence. Just start by tapping into the power of Mother Earth and ask her to assist you today in clearing out anything that is no longer in resonance with your highest good and deepest well-being. Tap into that infinite wall of unconditional love, deep compassion. Know radical forgiveness deep inside the crystal heart of Mother Earth.

Start by taking a deep breath into your chakra, allowing that high-frequency energy to move up from the tailbone, up the spine, touching, opening, balancing, and harmonizing all your chakras. Take a deep breath in. Allow that energy to move further up to your chest, moving around in the front, in the back of your heart. Deep breath in going higher up to the throat and the back of your neck. Another deep breath in moving upward, touching the space in between your eyebrows and feel the energy moving around in your head. Another deep breath and feel how the energy is moving up and it's now softly touching your crown. Another deep breath in and feel how the energy is gently exiting through the top of your head. Just imagine that you are breathing in from the foot upward to the crown. You feel that the energy is touching, opening, balancing, and harmonizing all of your chakras. Take a deep breath in from the foot up to the crown and see how the energy is softly exiting through the top of your head, cleansing and clearing your auric field to prepare you to release limiting beliefs in karmic agreements in all directions of time and space in this lifetime and all incarnations, past, present, and future on this planet in this reality, in all other dimensions or levels of existence. Take another deep breath in. Just relax. It feels so good to relax and know that you are taking charge of your life right now and power in your energetic support team to assist you today.

Take a deep breath in setting your intention, the power of your intentional attention, to call in your energetic support team. This can be your angels, your guides, power animals, your ancestors; maybe it's your inner child or your higher self, and feel that I feel how your energetic support team unconditionally loves you. Feel the love of your energetic support team that surrounds you right now and call upon Archangel Michael and Archangel Raphael if they are not yet present in this circle. Call these powerful angels in right now. Hurry Archangel Michael, Archangel Raphael, I asked you to be with me right now. Exhale.

Relaxing can call upon all the beings of love light and wisdom to assist you in this deep clearing process. They are here to remind you that you are on a divine assignment. You are showing up for this divine appointment with the help and support of your energetic support team and by the power of your intentional attention today. You are taking charge of your life right now. You are setting a strong intention to clear and break all karmic vows. You have the power to clear any and all negative energies on the deepest cellular level. Clearing your cell memory from multiple issues from multiple lifetimes, in this lifetime, and in past lives in this reality and all others, in all directions of time and space, past present, and future. So take another deep breath in. On the exhale, see yourself entering the space of tranquility and peace that resides eternally inside of you. Open yourself up to release the effects of fear that you may have observed in other dimensions and areas of time. Allow your energetic support team and the powerful Archangel Michael and Archangel Raphael to do all the work in the clearing. Invite them in and simply allow them to have full access to your cell memory, your heart center, and emotional body.

Take another deep breath in. Exhale and relax. Affirm I now release all pain and limiting beliefs that I may have acquired because of my experiences in any lifetime involving rejection, betrayal, abuse, inquisitions, persecution, abduction, humiliation, unrequited love, frustration and a stress of any kind.

Take a deep breath in, then exhale, relaxing. I forgive myself for any and all mistakes that I believe I have made with loved ones, including my partner, parents, siblings, and my children in this and any other lifetimes, in this reality and all other dimensions in all directions of time and space, past, present, and future. I forgive myself and choose a new timeline where I am free of this karmic agreement. I forgive myself for any aggressive behavior that I conducted towards others, any behavior that involves abuse, molestation, betrayal, rape, torture, prosecution.

Deep breath in. Exhale. I agree with this message. I forgive myself for any time I did not help another person in need. I forgive myself and choose a new timeline where I am free of this karmic agreement. I forgive myself, and I release all effects of my behavior regarding the abuse of my body: abortion, prostitution, smoking, excessive eating and drinking, drug-taking. I forgive myself for all the times when I ignored my intuition of a better judgment, and I hereby sever and break all the vows of poverty. I let go of these vows, and I release all effects of these vows I made in this and any other lifetimes, in this reality and all other dimensions, in all directions of time and space, past, present, and future. I hereby sever and break all the vows of celibacy. I let go of these vows, and I release all effects of these vows I made in this and any other lifetimes, in this reality and all other dimensions in all directions of time and space, past, present, and future. I hereby sever and break all the vows of suffering. I let go of these vows of suffering, and I release all effects of these vows I made in this and any other lifetimes, in this reality and all other dimensions, in all directions of time and space, past, present, and future. I hereby sever and break all the vows of any limiting beliefs that I may have acquired by being killed in any lifetime and in any dimension by drowning, burning, hanging, flooding, earthquakes, flying, crucifixion, falling, stabbing, beheading, insect bites, snakes, poisoning, bleeding to death, stoning, gunshots, explosions, tornadoes, hurricanes, plagues, disease, head wound, war, accidents, spontaneous combustion, suffocation, lancing, torture, starvation, any death connected to a pyramid, Atlantis, Lemuria, being smothered by quicksand, falling stones or debris, being sacrificed, being initiated, crimes of passion, jealousy, being trampled by animals, being eaten by animals, by Inquisition, humiliation, kidnapping, rape, robbed, or beaten.

Take a deep breath in. On the exhale, relax. I ask that all karma be balanced in all directions of time and space, past, present, and future, in relationships involving the soul who is my mother in this lifetime and the soul who is my father in this lifetime, the souls who have acted in the role of a legal guardian or step-parent in this lifetime, the souls who have been my lovers for spouses in this lifetime, the souls who have been my born are unborn children wanted or unwanted in this lifetime the souls who have been my born or unborn siblings in this lifetime, the souls who have been my stepchildren and children in this lifetime. I ask that all karma be balanced in all directions of time and space, past, present, and future. I ask that all karma be balanced with the souls who have been my employers, co-workers, customers, clients, students, and employees in this lifetime with the souls I went to school with: my teachers, principals, coaches, other students, and childhood friends. I ask that all karma be balanced with the souls of my loves. I ask that all karma be balanced in all directions of time and space, past, present, and future, with the souls who have been my friends in this lifetime, the souls in my pet animals in this lifetime, with the souls who have played a role of my prosecutors in this and other lifetimes. I asked that all karma be balanced in all directions of time and space with the souls who have been my rivals in this and other lifetimes, with the souls that I have yet to meet in this lifetime.

I acknowledged that I had made mistakes in my thinking in this and other lifetimes, and I understand that these mistakes originated in fear, which is an unreal basis for all decisions. I, therefore, release this and all fears, and I ask that all effects of my mistakes and fear-based thinking be forgiven and forgotten, but all involved in this lifetime and all lifetime's past, present, and future. I release the effect of all mistakes made in my childhood, made in my adolescence, made in my early adult years, made in recent years or made in the future. I release all effects of mistakes made in other lifetimes on this or any other planet, in this reality and all other dimensions, in all directions of time and space, past, present, and future. I take full responsibility for these mistakes, and I ask for intervention from all the beings of love, light, compassion, forgiveness, and wisdom so that I do not repeat them and stop this karmic cycle. I ask that all pain created by these mistakes be transformed and transmuted into lessons of growth and expansion and that all karma and everyone involved, be harmonized and balanced right now. I release, harmonize, and balance the Karma involved with every one of my romantic relationships in this and other lifetimes, on this or any other planet, in this reality and all other dimensions in all directions of time and space, past, present, and future. I release all effects of mistakes that I or others have made connected to romance, infatuation, passion, lust, sexuality, monogamy, infidelity, jealousy, impregnation, conception, childbirth, marriage. I am willing to release any unforgiveness I may be harboring on an unconscious level in my cell memory of the physical body, in my emotional body, or mind, connected to any romantic involvement like unrequited love, romantic betrayals, disappointments, arguments, control, and manipulation, breakups in all directions of time and space, past, present, and future.

Take a deep breath in, exhale, relaxing. Knowing that by releasing this pain, I am making space, clearing and cleaning, opening myself up to receive and accept healthy loving relationships into my life.

Take a deep breath in, then exhale, relax. I am willing to release all pain and suffering on a deep cell level connected with sexuality, including emotional abuse, blackmail, control, and manipulation in regards to sex; control and manipulation in regards to money, molestation, sexual assault, incest, rape, sadism, masochism, infidelity, sexual torture or abuse of any kind, pornography.

Take a deep breath in, exhale, relax. I am willing to release all pain and suffering on a deep cell level connected with sexual shaming afflicted by parents, siblings, lovers, spouses, friends, media, organized religion, teachers, medical personnel, or any other authority figures.

Take a deep breath in, exhale, relax. I now surround myself with a powerful shower of divine light, and I call upon fragments of my soul essence that have been left at places of my traumas. I call upon fragments of my soul essence that have been left with people with whom I have been involved. I call upon these fragments of my soul essence to be rejoined with me right now. I call upon these fragments of my soul essence to be returned to me now, entering through the divine light shower and being cleansed of all karmic imbalances, pain, and limiting beliefs. I call upon all these fragments of my soul essence to return to me right now.

Exhale, relax. I willingly clear all painful thoughts and feelings I hold about my body. I release, harmonize and stabilize all karma connected to my physical health right now. I transmute all pain into healthy lessons to grow and expand on a soul level, and I release the need to suffer in my body.

Take a deep breath in, relax. I commit to fully receive and accept all growth and expansion through joy and harmony, and I release all beliefs that I can only grow when I suffer or experience hardship or pain.

Take a deep breath in, exhale, relax. I release all beliefs that make me want to punish myself, and I asked my energetic support team to help me cleanse my thoughts of guilt and shame.

Take a deep breath in, exhale, relax. I replace these negative beliefs with the energy of unconditional love, radical forgiveness, and deep compassion, breathing in that energy.

Take a deep breath in, exhale, relax. I am willing to release all karma connected to cruel or unloving words that I or others have said about me. I recognize that these words come from the fear-based perspective of ego-personality, which is unloving in nature. I, therefore, commit to stop seeking love in approval from other people's ego, from their ego's perspective and personality, and to recognize the source of all true love, compassion, forgiveness, and approval instead, recognizing it as a source, as a part of the divine aspect of everyone I meet. I now ask Archangel Michael and Archangel Raphael and their team of angels to surround me with healing blue, purple, and green lights. I asked the Angels to disentangle me from all cords created from fear, control, and manipulation in any relationship, in this and any other lifetime, on this or any other planets, in this reality and all other dimensions, in all directions of time and space, past, present, and future. I ask Archangel Michael to cut all fear-based etheric cords and that any cord draining my energy lifeforce or enthusiasm be cut from me right now.

Take a deep breath in. I see, know, and feel within me a beautiful orb of brilliant diamond white light. I see, know, and feel this ball of light growing and warming me from the inside, and I command that this light fill up my physical body and the energy surrounding it, filling up my aura with this divine healing light. I now send divine light, filled with blessings of unconditional love, radical forgiveness, and deep compassion to everyone who has ever thought of me, seen me, read of me, heard of me, or met me in person or online. I send blessings of unconditional love, radical forgiveness, and deep compassion to everyone who will ever think of me, ever see me, ever read about me, ever hear about me, or ever meet me in person or online, be it on this or any other planet, in this reality and all other dimensions, in all directions of time and space, past, present, and future. I send blessings of unconditional love, radical forgiveness, and deep compassion to myself in all directions of time and space, embracing myself, sending myself these blessings as a child in this lifetime, reassuring myself that all is well and that all will continue to be well. I send blessings of unconditional love, radical forgiveness, and deep compassion to ease and erase all my childhood fears in all directions of time and space. I send blessings of unconditional love, radical forgiveness, and deep compassion to myself in other lifetimes, embracing myself, sending myself these blessings, reassuring myself that all is well and that all will continue to be well.

Take a deep breath in. My consciousness is now clear. My body is light and healthy. My heart is filled with love and radiant joy. I am free and I am happy. I am a powerful being of light sent here as a ray of happiness to bring sunshine to others. I allow this power to fully shine through me in all directions of time and space, in this and other lifetimes, on this and any other planets, in this reality and all other dimensions, past, present, and future right now.

.

CHAPTER 11. AKASHIC PRAYERS: CONNECT WITH YOUR SOUL FOR THE HIGHEST GOOD OF ALL

Akashic Prayer is a way to pray for your own life, other people's lives and the world. Praying with Akasha means that you are praying without words, asking God or Spirit for help in an area of need. This type of prayer can be done at any time and in any place. The power of this type of prayer is enormous because it sends out a request into the universe on behalf of yourself and others who may not know they need help but do want healing from their pain or suffering.

Praying with Akasha also has a big impact on the environment because it brings peace and balance to nature, including plants, animals, insects, and birds.

With Akasha, you're able to do two things: pray for something or someone and ask to see the Akashic Record by seeing yourself going into a vision and traveling there.

Making an Akashic Prayer
A small and simple prayer that does not require words can be made with a few steps. The first is to close your eyes and take a few deep breaths, the second is to visualize the person you are praying for, and the third is to say, "I am offering this prayer for

(name of person)." You can offer a prayer for yourself or someone else. This type of prayer doesn't need to be set in any specific time or space either. It could be done anywhere at any time as long as it's giving love and support from you to another person.

DAILY PRAYER FOR ALIGNMENT AND MEDITATION

If you're asking for help with something, it's important to affirm that you are ready to receive this help. You want to become aware of what is in alignment in your life and also clear yourself at the same time from any negative influences. This prayer will do both: open up your heart while clearing out any negative influence.

Write down your prayer when you're finished and place it on your altar or in a location where you will see it every morning. This is an important prayer for anyone who wants to open their heart up and receive guidance without any blockages at the same time. If you find yourself going through a challenging moment, never think that there isn't help available to you. You only need to ask, and you will receive assistance from the universe immediately.

You can do this prayer in a quiet place or your thoughts as you go through your day. The only requirement is that you do it every morning to open up yourself for a positive and productive day:

I ask right now to be connected with the _____ (spiritual guidance) so I may hear the words that reflect the highest and best in my life. I ask to know how this day will unfold to create a positive outcome for me. I bring into awareness all of my blessings and gifts and turn away from any negativity or distractions so that I may be free to make the right choices and decisions for myself today.

PRAYER FOR SELF-HEALING

This is an extremely powerful prayer when said first thing upon awakening. It will help clear any negative energies from the past day while opening up your heart for a positive new day.

Read it aloud, write it down, and put it in a place where you will see this every morning upon waking up. This is an excellent prayer that works for anyone who wants to be healed or achieve a goal; the steps involved are very easy to follow. Keep saying this prayer each morning until you receive your goal or desire. Be aware that this could happen quickly or take months. It all depends on what is in your highest good.

This prayer can be written down and read aloud when you need guidance or healing for yourself. It is most effective if said while sitting with your eyes closed:

My heart feels a deep desire to be _____ (fill in the blank). I am ready right now, without any hesitation, to receive from the universe all that I need to become the person I am meant to be. _____ (fill in the blank) is my highest goal and purpose, and with this prayer, I ask for guidance on how best to achieve my dreams.

I ask now for all of the wisdom, energy and love from God / Spirit so that I may awaken every morning to the truth of who I am. _____ (fill in the blank) is my greatest gift and I will share this with all of mankind today.

I ask that this prayer be filled with light, love and peace so that it may radiate through me to bless others too. Thank you for answering my call for help. Please guide and bless me with love, wisdom, guidance and spiritual awareness so that I may be led on my path to become _____ (fill in the blank).

SHARING YOUR BLESSINGS WITH OTHERS

This prayer can be repeated every morning upon awakening or whenever you feel guided to say it again. It helps those who are seeking assistance to find a better place in life.

One of the major benefits of prayer is that once you have received help for yourself, you can now share your blessings with others. This prayer will show you how:

I feel so blessed and thank God/Spirit for _____ and I ask now to share this blessing with others. My mind is filled with such wonderful thoughts, and my heart overflows with love that I may be able to get my message out there so that all who need help will find it. Thank you, God/Spirit, for allowing me to serve humanity positively every day. My goal is to be the best person I can be to help improve the quality of human life on earth today.

God/Spirit, please send me all who wish to hear my message and bless them with healing or assistance somehow. Please guide me in how I am best able to bring forth these blessings to humanity. Thank you for knowing me and helping me become the person I am meant to be. This prayer is now complete, in God/Spirit we trust.

PRAYER OF SELF-LOVE

This prayer aims to help the person be in a place where they can accept love from others. This prayer would also work for someone who has been wounded, abused and hurt so many times that they are not sure if anyone can love them anymore. To ask God/Spirit to shine light into those darkest moments to help find strength and courage.

When we say these words aloud or think them inside our minds, it generates the universe as a pure giving force with no judgments about whether or not one deserves their prayers answered.

My prayer is to accept each day as a new beginning. May I choose today to be positive and filled with purpose. I will recall the past without regret but with gratitude for having learned how I can love myself more in the present so that my future may be brighter. Let all the goodness of life flow through me, like a gentle stream, shining brightly. May I honor God, others and myself above all else today by making a positive difference wherever I decide to focus my thoughts and actions.

I am _____. I love and accept myself, just as I am.

I am _____. I Am enough. I will not carry the burden of judgment or criticism.

I am _____. I am worthy and deserve unconditional love and happiness.

I am _____. I release my past attachments and behaviors that no longer serve me and choose to embrace the power within myself.

I am _____. I release my fears and open myself up to unconditional love, joy, peace and happiness.

I am _____. I see myself as a powerful being of light and love who is worthy of all goodness.

PRAYER OF RECEIVING GUIDANCE

The purpose of this prayer is to ask God or Spirit for a message of guidance every night before going to bed. This prayer can be done in three different ways: 1) saying it aloud, 2) repeating it silently in your mind or 3) writing it down. It's important to make sure you are clear about the type of guidance you want and need to be effective.

I am _____. I ask that my Guide and the spirit guides of this group hold me in their loving care as we open up to receive divine inspiration, healing energy and clarity of mind.

I am now opening myself to clear thoughts, spiritual knowledge, and inspiration from the Divine within me. As I continue with this process, I am also open to receiving divine healing in my body, mind and emotions.

By this divine process of intuitive thinking, we are given the inspiration, knowledge, love, and happiness required for our highest good. We ask these things from God, the Divine within us, and all guides present with us now. So be it.

As we open ourselves to intuitive thinking and spiritual inspiration, let us release all negative thoughts that no longer serve us. Let there be room for a new level of insight and understanding within our minds.

Let the energy of love surround us now in this space. We ask for God's divine protection as we listen to those things which will help us in our lives today and in the future. We ask this from

God, the Divine within us and all Guides present at this time. So be it.

Now that we have asked for insight and understanding into matters of our greatest concern, let us all open ourselves to accept spiritual guidance from our souls as well as from the souls of those who are present in this room now. These energies will bless us, offer insight into our current problems, and help us make truly right decisions. I also ask that my guardian angel come forward to protect me from all harm and negativity as we engage in this intuitive process. So be it.

PRAYER OF FORGIVENESS OF OTHERS

The purpose of this prayer is to help release forgiveness from your heart for others who have hurt you in a way that is no longer serving your higher good. It can be used when thinking about specific people or all people at once.

Forgiveness is not something that you give out of obligation, but rather because it allows us to heal emotionally and move on from things that might be holding us back. We all know people who have hurt or mistreated us at some point in life, but this does not mean we need to carry those feelings forward with us day after day and year after year. Forgiveness is a powerful tool that allows us to release the negative feelings of being hurt and mistreated by another. This forgiveness prayer can be done at any time and in any place, whether you're alone or with a group of people.

However, it's most effective if all who are present for the prayer are doing it simultaneously as a group meditation. If this is not possible due to logistics and other factors, then each person can take the prayer to heart and apply it in their way.

My family and loved ones, I forgive you. I know that we are all connected through the Akashic Records, and we need not worry about others because they are taking care of themselves. This is what I am doing from now on—loving myself with grace, peace and understanding. Forgiveness should never be hard when we come from this space of understanding. I live in harmony with every living creature on Earth, and I thank you for the blessings that have been given to me. Blessed be!

PRAYER TO CLEAR OTHERS' ENERGY

This prayer can be used when you feel a sensation (physical, emotional, or mental) that may be from someone else. Empathetic absorption is done to understand others or heal their pain. People come into our energy field to understand us, to receive physical energy or sometimes to communicate with us. This unconscious action is not a service to us. When we allow others to fill our energy field, it is almost impossible to be centered on our Soul Path, as it's hard to know what that is.

Mother/Father/Goddess/God, please assist me in clearing and releasing all outside energies that are in my body, aura and energy field. Please send them back to the person from which they came, or send them to the Divine Source to be recycled for the highest good of all. I am filled with the purest energy and highest vibration I can now hold.

Daily Prayer to Clear Entities and Energy Patterns
This prayer may be used personally to release any energy that interferes with your evolution and guidance. You may also use

it for other people if they desire assistance. Entities often have contracts with us, and you may go into your Akashic Record and receive information about these contracts to finish the clearing for good.

I call Archangel Michael and his legions alongside the Akashic Beings of Light and Divine Source. Please surround me with your Light and Love and keep me protected and safe as I order the release and clearing of all energies, interference, thoughts, feelings, patterns, programming, and imprinting across all time and space, in all dimensions and levels, and all places and planes that are not in alignment with my Highest and Best Akashic Blueprint. You are to leave my body, mind, and energy field. Now and forever!

DAILY PRAYER TO ASSIST FORWARD MOTION

This prayer may be used to release any energy that holds you back from your evolution.

Mother, Father, Goddess, God, please release the ties that bind me. Help me expand outside of time and space to clear and release any energy trapped in the past, from the beginning of time until this present moment. Please help me gather my highest energy to have the impetus to move forward on my soul path, fulfilling my soul purpose. So it is. Blessed Be.

PRAYER FOR CREATING YOUR DREAMS

This prayer is perfect in conjunction with the prayer "To Assist forward Motion" or to use alone to focus on your talents.

I am clear. I am focused. I am ready to do whatever it takes to make my dreams come true. I know that my clarity with the assistance of Akashic Records creates miracles in my life. I am seen, heard and recognized for the gifts and talents I offer. The universe conspires with me to make magic happen, and my dreams come true. So it is. Blessed Be.

DAILY PRAYER OF CREATING HEAVEN ON EARTH

This prayer may be used to remind us that there is great power in our bodies and our souls, and the two together is one of the easiest ways to manifest now.

As I integrate the power of the soul with the power of the body, I can manifest with ease and grace here on Earth. I am a Creator Being with a purpose. I am creating Heaven on Earth now. So it is. Blessed Be.

PRAYER FOR A STRONG SENSE OF AT-ONENESS WITH ALL LIVING CREATURES

We have a strong sense of connection and at-one-ness with all living things. This prayer may be used to enhance that sense of oneness.

I am one with all Living Creatures in the Universe. We are the same. We are connected by Divine Source, and we act as One to fulfill the purpose of life. So it is. Blessed Be.

PRAYER TO REMOVE NEGATIVE ENERGY

This prayer is to remind us to remove all negativity from our body and energy field. It pulls all negative energy back into the earth, dissipating and being harmlessly reabsorbed by the earth. This prayer is also perfect for clearing your home and office.

Remove all negative energy, emotions, thoughts, imprinting and memories that are not mine or of the highest good from this place here and now. You are to leave my body, mind and soul forever! So it is. Blessed Be.

PRAYER TO RELEASE INSECURITIES

This prayer is best done in a quiet space. It may be used as often as needed.

I ask that the energies of insecurity, fear and doubt be removed from my consciousness now and for all time. I know that I am loved beyond measure, and I love myself completely with no limits or boundaries on this love. So it is. Blessed Be.

PRAYER TO RELEASE FEAR

This prayer is best done in a quiet space. It may be used as often as needed.

I release all fears I hold within me now and forever! I know that Divine Source will only send me experiences, life lessons, and opportunities aligned with my highest path. And I am grateful for the experience, even if it appears difficult. I release all fear and feelings of unworthiness from my heart, mind, body and soul now and forever! So it is. Blessed Be.

***

Akashic Prayer is a way to pray for your own life, other people's lives and the world. Praying with Akasha means that you are praying without words, asking God or Spirit for help in an area of need. This type of prayer can be done at any time and in any place. The power of this type of prayer is enormous because it sends out a request into the universe on behalf of yourself and others who may not know they need help but do want healing from their pain or suffering. Even if you have trouble finding peace within your body, mind, heart, and soul, this form of meditation will work wonders to connect to Divine Source and manifest what we want in our lives through spiritual energy. The only limitation we have is the one that creates when we don't believe or trust in our cosmic potential.

.

CONCLUSION

The Akashic Records are believed by some to be records that of all humans go through in order for them to learn and grow on their journey.

Why do people believe in these Records? What exactly are the Records and who created them? Are they a way for our souls to develop us on how we should live on Earth, or something else completely different? Why do some people not believe in them? And what does believing in the Akashic Records mean to them?

I believe that the Akashic Records are our guide to live well on this earth and that they tell us how we should be good people in order to have a better life, but everyone is entitled to their own point of view.

The ancient texts say that humans who lived thousands of years ago knew about the Akashic Records and they were their guide to live on Earth, that these ancient people believed in them and followed the guidelines given by them. But as time passed different religions came about, all with a different story of how these records came into existence, so this is what created confusion in our society about how we should view the Akashic Records.

Today most people don't know about the Akashic Records and they believe that these records are something like a video camera that records everything we do in our lives. But there are some people who claim to have been able to go inside the Akashic Realm and see how it was created, from what I understand they say that this is something spiritual.

These Records don't tell us how we should live our lives and what kind of a person we should be like because it all depends on the individual, but I believe that this book tells us how to become better people just as the ancient texts say. No matter what a person believes in, whatever religion we follow, the Akashic Records are always telling us that we should be good and kind people in order to receive the good things in life.

I believe that the Akashic Records are a way for humans to travel through their lives with peace and love and it gives them guidance.

The Akashic Records have been present since ancient times but because of different religions people have started to believe that they are something else, mostly they think that these records are like a video camera.

This is the explanation of how I view the Akashic Records and what I personally believe, but everyone is entitled to their own opinion.

I think that believing in these books can help us have a better life if we use this information as a guide for how we should be good people who live with peace and love.

The Akashic Records are believed by some to be a place where the human memory of all events and emotions ever experienced in the history of humanity exists. This includes the time before birth, past live times, alternative lives, parallel universes and pure consciousness. The energy of our thoughts and emotions contained in these Records (allegedly) can be read, viewed, or searched from the Akashic Records.

The Records were supposedly created by a civilization before the ancient civilizations that we know of today. Many individuals believe they are similar to a large computer database which contains all past, present and future events for each person on earth, and possibly on other planets as well.

These Records are also believed to be the source of divine guidance for the right path in life for each person. They supposedly contain our spiritual learning lessons from all lives lived (past, present, and future). I believe that we choose these lessons for ourselves before birth because we want to learn more about the spiritual side of things.

The Records are supposedly located at the astral level and can be viewed there with advanced psychic ability. There have been many cases in history times when people were able to view or read these records.

Akashic Records are our guide to live a good life, the ancient texts say that this is a gift that we have been given to help us through our lives. So, use the knowledge of this book to make better choices in your life.

The Records contain the details from all of our lives and if we use this information as a guide for how to become better people then I believe that life will be easier. All it takes is one person who sees these things in a positive way and thinks that life can be changed so let me say this to you, my friend: I believe that the Akashic Records can make this world a better place.

The Records tell us how our life will be in the near future but also how it will turn out if we don't choose to see this information as important and decide not to change our ways. This is why we should learn from them and live a better life.

A REVIEW WOULD HELP!

I hope you loved this book and found it worth your time. If so, I would be forever grateful if you could leave me a review on Amazon to help other readers find my work. The marketplaces are tough these days - which is why reviews really make a difference for authors like myself who want their published works seen by the masses! It only takes 30 seconds of your time but definitely makes an important impact in helping emerging writers get more attention from potential buyers out there looking for new books to read.

Thank you again for reading my book, happy reviewing!

In case you enjoyed the notions or learned something useful from what I shared, please post an honest review online visiting the following link:

LEAVE A REVIEW HERE:

>> https://swiy.io/AkashicRecordsMGReview<<

OR scan the QR code with your phone*:

The above link is made for amazon.com. If you buy the book from other marketplaces, kindly leave us a review by visiting the review page in your respective marketplace. Thank you

BONUS: FREE AUDIO VERSION

OF THIS BOOK

If you love listening to audiobooks on-the-go or would enjoy a narration as you read along, I have great news for you. You can download the audiobook version of *this book* for FREE just by signing up for a FREE 30-day Audible trial!

VISIT THE FOLLOWING LINK:

https://swiy.io/AkashicRecordsAudio

OR scan the QR code with your phone:

Bonus: Free Workbook - Value $~~$12.99~~

To help you take some time for yourself and reflect on what actions to take while reading the book, I have prepared a Free Workbook with some key questions to ask yourself and a To Do List which can help you get deeper into the topic of this book. I hope this helps!

You can find the Free Workbook by visiting
>> https://swiy.io/AkashicRecordsMGWorkbook<<

OR scan the QR Code with your phone's camera

BONUS: FREE BOOK – VALUE

~~$14.99~~

As a way of saying thank you for downloading this book, I'm offering the eBook *RUNES FOR BEGINNERS A Pagan Guide to Reading and Casting the Elder Futhark Rune Stones for Divination, Norse Magic, and Modern Witchcraft* for FREE.

In *Runes for Beginners*, Melissa Gomes reveals some of the most interesting and secret aspects of how to perform Runes Reading and Runes Casting. You will discover new insights into the magical word of Runes and how to link with them.

Click Below for the Free Gift OR Scan the QR Code with your phone
>> https://swiy.io/RunesFreeBook<<

Printed in Great Britain
by Amazon

28552791R00084